GOODSON MUMBA

Wisdom in the Workplace
Philosophical Perspectives on Management

Copyright © 2025 by Goodson Mumba

All rights reserved. No part of this publication may be reproduced, stored, or transmitted in any form or by any means, electronic, mechanical, photocopying, recording, scanning, or otherwise without written permission from the publisher. It is illegal to copy this book, post it to a website, or distribute it by any other means without permission.

First edition

ISBN: 9798334807778

This book was professionally typeset on Reedsy. Find out more at reedsy.com

Contents

Preface	iv
Acknowledgments	vi
Dedication	vii
Disclaimer	viii
Chapter 1: Introduction to Philosophical Management	1
Chapter 2: Ethics in Management	15
Chapter 3: The Philosophy of Leadership	36
Chapter 4: The Role of Purpose in Management	52
Chapter 5: Decision-Making and Rationality	68
Chapter 6: Justice and Fairness in the Workplace	84
Chapter 7: Corporate Social Responsibility (CSR)	101
Chapter 8: Sustainability and Ethical Management	118
Chapter 9: The Philosophy of Work and Labor	135
Chapter 10: Organizational Culture and Ethics	153
Chapter 11: Communication and Philosophy	173
Chapter 12: Innovation and Creativity	191
Chapter 13: Power and Authority in Management	208
Chapter 14: Globalization and Management	226
Chapter 15: The Future of Philosophical Management	243
About the Author	259

Preface

In the constantly evolving landscape of modern business, the quest for effective management practices has never been more critical. As organizations strive for excellence, they often turn to established methodologies, strategic frameworks, and cutting-edge technologies. Yet, amidst this pursuit, the profound insights offered by philosophical inquiry are frequently overlooked. This book, "Wisdom in the Workplace: Philosophical Perspectives on Management," seeks to bridge that gap by exploring how the timeless principles of philosophy can enrich contemporary management practices.

My journey into the intersection of philosophy and management began a decade ago when, as a young management consultant, I found myself grappling with the deeper questions underlying business decisions. What constitutes ethical leadership? How can we balance profit with purpose? What role does wisdom play in decision-making? These questions, I realized, could not be fully addressed through traditional business education alone. They required a philosophical lens.

In "Wisdom in the Workplace," we embark on a journey through the foundational concepts of philosophy as they relate to various facets of management. From ethics and leadership to organizational culture and innovation, each chapter delves into philosophical theories and their practical applications. Through case studies, reflective questions, and actionable insights, this book aims to provide a comprehensive guide for managers, leaders, and anyone interested in enhancing their understanding of the philosophical dimensions of their work.

The insights presented in this book are not merely academic. They are drawn from real-world experiences, extensive research, and the collective wisdom of thinkers who have shaped our understanding of human nature, ethics, and leadership. By integrating these perspectives into management practices, we can foster more ethical, innovative, and resilient organizations.

As you read through the chapters, I invite you to reflect on your own experiences and consider how philosophical wisdom can inform your approach to management. Whether you are a seasoned executive, an emerging leader, or a student of business, I hope this book serves as a valuable resource, sparking thoughtful dialogue and inspiring meaningful change in your professional life.

Thank you for joining me on this exploration of wisdom in the workplace. May the philosophical perspectives presented here guide you toward more enlightened and effective management practices.

Sincerely,
Goodson Mumba

Acknowledgments

I would like to eternally and gratefully acknowledge the Almighty God for the infinite intelligence from His universal mind where we draw from all that we come to know and are yet to know. May I also acknowledge and thank everyone that has played a part in my journey of life in terms of spiritual, moral, emotional and material support.

Dedication

I extend my sincerest gratitude to my beloved wife, Edith Mumba, and our children, Angelina, Lubuto, Letticia, Lulumbi, and Butusho, for their unwavering support and understanding throughout the conception, writing, and eventual publication of this book, despite the sacrifices and challenges they endured.

Disclaimer

This book is a work of fiction. Names, characters, businesses, places, events, and incidents are either the products of the author's imagination or used in a fictitious manner. Any resemblance to actual persons, living or dead, or actual events is purely coincidental.

Chapter 1: Introduction to Philosophical Management

Definition and Importance of Philosophy in Management

The boardroom of Apex Global Consulting buzzed with quiet anticipation. The executive team had gathered for a special session, intrigued by the unusual agenda item: "Philosophy in Management." As the clock struck nine, the door swung open, and in walked Michael, the newly appointed CEO, known for his unconventional yet profoundly effective leadership style.

"Good morning, everyone," Michael began, his voice calm yet commanding. He placed a well-worn leather-bound book on the table, its cover embossed with gold letters spelling out "Philosophical Reflections."

"Today," he continued, "we embark on a journey that will transform how we lead and manage. Our focus is not on the latest market trends or technological innovations, but on the timeless wisdom of philosophy."

The team exchanged curious glances, unsure of what to expect.

"Let's start with a simple question," Michael said, leaning forward. "What is philosophy, and why should it matter in management?"

He paused, allowing the weight of his question to settle. "Philosophy," he explained, "is the study of fundamental questions about existence, knowledge, values, reason, mind, and language. It provides a framework for critical thinking, ethical reasoning, and reflective practice."

Michael walked over to the whiteboard and wrote three key words: **"Existence," "Knowledge," and "Values."**

"Consider this," he continued. "Every decision we make as leaders our organization's existence, shapes our collective knowledge, and reflects our values. By integrating philosophical principles into our management practices, we can navigate these complexities with greater clarity and purpose."

He turned to face his team, his eyes shining with conviction. "Philosophy helps us question our assumptions, challenge our biases, and explore different perspectives. It equips us with the tools to make ethical decisions, foster a culture of continuous learning, and lead with integrity."

Michael glanced at the book on the table. "Take Socrates, for example. His method of inquiry, known as the Socratic method, is about asking probing questions to stimulate critical thinking and illuminate ideas. Imagine applying this to our strategy meetings—encouraging open dialogue, questioning our assumptions, and arriving at more robust solutions."

The room grew silent as the team absorbed Michael's words, the power of his vision beginning to take root.

"But philosophy is not just about abstract ideas," Michael continued, his voice growing more passionate. "It's about practical application. Aristotle's concept of virtue ethics, for instance, teaches us to cultivate virtues such as courage, honesty, and compassion. These virtues are not just personal traits; they are essential qualities of effective leaders."

He looked around the room, making eye contact with each team member. "By embracing philosophical thinking, we can elevate our leadership, make more thoughtful decisions, and create a workplace where every individual thrives."

The team members nodded, a sense of excitement and possibility filling the room.

"So, as we embark on this journey," Michael concluded, "let's commit to exploring these philosophical insights and integrating them into our daily practices. Together, we will not only achieve success but also create a legacy of wisdom and integrity."

With that, the room erupted in applause, the team energized and inspired by Michael's vision. The journey into the realm of philosophical management had begun, promising to reshape their understanding of leadership and unlock new potentials within themselves and their organization.

Historical Overview of Philosophy in Business

The applause gradually subsided, leaving an air of eager anticipation hanging in the boardroom of Apex Global Consulting. Michael smiled, appreciating the team's enthusiasm. He knew the journey into philosophical management had just begun, and there was much more to explore.

"Now," Michael continued, "let's take a step back in time and understand the historical relationship between philosophy and business. This isn't a new idea; it's a rich tradition that has influenced leaders and thinkers for centuries."

He clicked a button on the remote, and a projection screen descended from the ceiling, displaying an image of ancient Athens. "Our journey begins with the ancient Greeks. Philosophers like Socrates, Plato, and Aristotle laid the groundwork for ethical thinking and critical inquiry."

Michael pointed to a statue of Aristotle. "Aristotle, for instance, emphasized the importance of ethics and virtue in leadership. He believed that the purpose of life was to achieve 'eudaimonia'—a state of flourishing and well-being. For Aristotle, a good life was intertwined with the practice of virtues, which is directly relevant to how we lead our organizations today."

The screen transitioned to a medieval scene, depicting monasteries and scholars. "In the Middle Ages," Michael narrated, "philosophy and business intersected in the form of Scholasticism. Thinkers like Thomas Aquinas integrated Aristotelian ethics with Christian theology, influencing the moral foundations of trade and commerce. These scholars debated just pricing, fair trade, and the ethical responsibilities of merchants."

Next, the screen showed the bustling markets of Renaissance Europe. "The Renaissance period brought about a revival of classical thought. Niccolò Machiavelli, often misunderstood, provided keen insights into power dynamics and leadership in 'The Prince.' While some of his advice was controversial, it sparked essential discussions about the ethical use of power and the nature of leadership."

The image then shifted to the Industrial Revolution, with factories and steam engines. "The 18th and 19th centuries saw the rise of capitalism, and philosophers like Adam Smith explored the moral implications of free markets. In 'The

Wealth of Nations,' Smith introduced the concept of the 'invisible hand,' but he also wrote about ethics in 'The Theory of Moral Sentiments,' emphasizing empathy and the importance of ethical behavior in economic systems."

Michael paused, allowing the team to absorb the breadth of history. "Fast forward to the 20th century," he continued, as the screen displayed images of modern-day corporate leaders and iconic companies. "Philosophy continued to influence business thought through the works of Peter Drucker, who emphasized management as a liberal art, combining scientific methods with humanistic values. Drucker believed that a manager's role was not just to optimize resources but to cultivate a thriving organizational culture."

He then pointed to an image of contemporary thinkers. "Today, scholars and leaders continue to draw on philosophical insights to address complex issues like corporate social responsibility, sustainability, and ethical leadership. The works of philosophers such as John Rawls and Amartya Sen provide frameworks for justice and fairness in business practices."

Michael turned off the projector, bringing the focus back to himself. "The historical relationship between philosophy and business is a testament to the enduring relevance of philosophical thought. By understanding this rich tradition, we can better appreciate the depth and complexity of our own challenges and make more informed, ethical decisions."

He looked around the room, seeing the intrigue and understanding in the faces of his team. "As we move forward, let's remember that we are part of this long and noble tradition. By integrating philosophical insights into our management practices, we are not just leading our company; we are contributing to a legacy of thoughtful, ethical leadership."

With that, the team felt a renewed sense of purpose, ready to delve deeper into the philosophical perspectives that would guide their journey. The fusion of history, philosophy, and business had set the stage for a transformative approach to leadership, promising a future where wisdom and integrity would lead the way.

Key Philosophical Theories and Relevant to Management

The room settled into a contemplative silence, the weight of historical insights still hanging in the air. Michael, sensing the team's readiness to delve deeper, walked back to the center of the room, the soft click of his shoes the only sound breaking the quiet.

"Now," he began, his voice steady and inviting, "let's explore some key philosophical theories and how they directly apply to management. These theories will provide us with frameworks to navigate our daily challenges and opportunities with greater wisdom."

He clicked the remote, and the screen lit up with the image of an ancient Greek temple. "We'll start with the Greek philosophers. Aristotle's 'Virtue Ethics' focuses on the character of the individual. It's about cultivating virtues—courage, temperance, wisdom, and justice—that enable us to lead ethical lives. In management, this translates to leading by example and fostering a culture of integrity and moral excellence."

Michael moved to the next slide, which displayed a scale of justice. "From the realm of modern philosophy, we have Immanuel Kant and his theory of 'Deontological Ethics.' Kant

CHAPTER 1: INTRODUCTION TO PHILOSOPHICAL MANAGEMENT

emphasized the importance of duty and adherence to moral principles. He argued that actions are morally right if they are done out of duty and follow universal laws. For us, this means establishing and adhering to a strong ethical code within our organization, ensuring that our actions are guided by principles, not just outcomes."

He clicked again, and the screen showed a group of people in deep discussion. "Next, we have Utilitarianism, developed by Jeremy Bentham and John Stuart Mill. This theory suggests that the best action is the one that maximizes overall happiness or utility. In a management context, this means making decisions that aim to benefit the greatest number of stakeholders—employees, customers, shareholders, and the community."

The screen changed to a scene of a peaceful countryside, with people meditating under trees. "Eastern philosophies also offer profound insights. Take, for example, Confucianism, which emphasizes the importance of relationships, respect, and harmony. Confucius taught that good governance starts with self-cultivation and extends to family, community, and the state. In management, this underscores the value of building strong, respectful relationships and creating a harmonious workplace."

Michael looked around the room, ensuring the team was following. He then clicked again, revealing an image of a stoic figure standing tall amidst chaos. "The Stoic philosophers, such as Marcus Aurelius and Epictetus, offer another valuable perspective. Stoicism teaches us to focus on what we can control and accept what we cannot. It emphasizes resilience, emotional intelligence, and the importance of maintaining inner peace. For leaders, Stoicism provides tools to manage stress, stay calm under pressure, and inspire others through composed, thoughtful action."

The screen then displayed an image of a diverse group of people in a modern office setting. "Lastly, we have contemporary theories like John Rawls' 'Theory of Justice,' which introduces the concept of fairness as justice. Rawls argues for the 'veil of ignorance'—a method for determining the morality of issues. In management, this means creating fair policies and practices that consider the needs of all employees, promoting equity and inclusivity."

Michael turned off the projector, the room returning to its natural light. "These philosophical theories provide us with a diverse toolkit. They help us think critically about our decisions, understand the ethical dimensions of our actions, and strive to lead with wisdom and integrity."

He looked at each team member, his eyes reflecting a mix of challenge and encouragement. "As we integrate these theories into our management practices, let's remember that philosophy isn't just about abstract ideas—it's about practical application. It's about making our organization not just a place of work, but a community where individuals can thrive, innovate, and find meaning."

The team sat in thoughtful silence, the weight of Michael's words sinking in. They realized that their journey into philosophical management was not just about adopting new ideas, but about transforming their approach to leadership, infusing it with depth, ethical rigor, and a commitment to the greater good.

With renewed determination, they prepared to embark on this path, guided by the timeless wisdom of the world's greatest thinkers, ready to reshape their organization and themselves in the process.

Objectives and Scope of the Book

The room's atmosphere was electric with curiosity and reflection as Michael paused, allowing the profound insights of key philosophical theories to resonate with his team. He knew the next step was to outline the purpose and scope of their journey, encapsulating the essence of what they were about to explore together.

"Now that we've laid a philosophical foundation," Michael began, his voice steady and earnest, "let's turn our attention to the objectives and scope of this book, 'Wisdom in the Workplace: Philosophical Perspectives on Management.'"

The projector clicked on once more, displaying the book's title in elegant script against a backdrop of interwoven gears, symbolizing the intricate connection between philosophy and management.

"Our primary objective," Michael explained, "is to bridge the gap between ancient wisdom and modern management practices. This book is not just a collection of theories but a practical guide to applying philosophical insights to enhance our leadership, decision-making, and organizational culture."

He clicked to the next slide, which highlighted four main objectives.

"First," Michael said, pointing to the slide, "we aim to cultivate ethical leadership. By integrating philosophical principles, we want to foster a leadership style that prioritizes integrity, empathy, and moral courage. This means leading by example and creating an environment where ethical considerations are at the forefront of our decision-making processes."

He moved to the second point. "Second, we seek to enhance critical thinking and problem-solving skills. Philosophy teaches us to question assumptions, analyze complex issues from multiple perspectives, and develop well-reasoned solutions. In the fast-paced world of business, these skills are invaluable."

The third objective appeared on the screen. "Third, we strive to promote a culture of continuous learning and personal growth. Philosophy encourages lifelong learning and self-improvement. By adopting this mindset, we can inspire our employees to constantly seek knowledge, challenge themselves, and grow both personally and professionally."

Finally, the fourth objective lit up. "And fourth, we want to build a resilient and adaptive organization. Philosophical teachings on resilience, such as those from Stoicism, can help us navigate uncertainty and change with grace and fortitude. This will enable us to stay grounded and focused, even in the face of adversity."

Michael turned off the projector, stepping closer to his team, making the conversation more personal. "The scope of this book is broad but intentionally so. We will explore various philosophical traditions—Western, Eastern, ancient, and modern. We'll examine how their insights can be applied to different facets of management, including leadership, ethics, innovation, and work-life balance."

He paused, ensuring his words resonated deeply. "This journey is not about finding easy answers but about asking the right questions. It's about cultivating wisdom in our workplace, making decisions that reflect our highest values, and creating an organization where every individual feels valued and inspired."

CHAPTER 1: INTRODUCTION TO PHILOSOPHICAL MANAGEMENT

Michael looked around the room, meeting each person's gaze. "Our journey through 'Wisdom in the Workplace' will be both challenging and rewarding. It requires an open mind, a reflective heart, and a commitment to integrating these insights into our daily practices. But together, we can transform not just our organization, but ourselves, and in doing so, make a meaningful impact on the world around us."

The team sat in thoughtful silence, the weight of their shared mission settling in. They were not just embarking on a professional journey but a philosophical quest for wisdom, integrity, and excellence in the workplace.

With a sense of shared purpose and newfound determination, they prepared to delve deeper into the pages of "Wisdom in the Workplace," ready to uncover the profound connections between philosophy and management that would guide them toward a future of enlightened leadership and ethical success.

How to Apply Philosophical Concepts to Management Practices

The room was charged with a mix of anticipation and reflection as Michael's words sank in. The executives at Apex Global Consulting were not just listening; they were beginning to see the contours of a new kind of leadership emerging. Michael knew that to solidify their understanding, he needed to make the application of philosophical concepts concrete and actionable.

"Now," Michael said, his voice confident and engaging, "let's talk about how we can apply these philosophical concepts to our management practices. This is where theory meets reality."

He clicked the remote, and the screen displayed a practical framework: **"Applying Philosophy to Management: A Step-by-Step Guide."**

"First," Michael began, "we start with **self-reflection**. Philosophy teaches us the importance of knowing ourselves. Take a few minutes each day to reflect on your actions and decisions. Ask yourself: What were my motivations? Did I act according to my values? How could I improve?"

He paused, allowing the team to visualize this practice in their daily routines. "For instance, consider the Socratic method. It's about questioning and dialogue. In our meetings, let's make it a habit to ask probing questions. Challenge assumptions, encourage debate, and explore different viewpoints. This will lead to more robust and well-thought-out decisions."

The next slide showed a diverse group of employees engaged in a collaborative discussion. "Second," Michael continued, "we focus on **ethical decision-making**. Use Kantian ethics as a guide. Before making a decision, ask yourself: Is this action universally acceptable? Would I want all companies to act this way? This will help us ensure our decisions are just and fair."

He saw the team nodding, understanding the power of principled decision-making. "And don't forget Utilitarianism. We must consider the consequences of our actions and strive to achieve the greatest good for the greatest number. When planning a new policy or strategy, think about its impact on all stakeholders—employees, customers, the community, and the environment."

Michael clicked again, revealing an image of a serene garden, symbolizing balance and harmony. "Third, let's integrate **balance and resilience** into our work culture. From Stoicism, we learn to focus on what we can control and accept what we cannot. Teach this to your teams. During stressful projects, remind them to concentrate on their efforts, not the outcomes."

He moved closer to the team, making his next point more personal. "Encourage practices like mindfulness and meditation, drawn from Eastern philosophies. These can help our employees maintain inner peace and clarity, even in high-pressure situations. Create spaces and opportunities for them to unwind and reflect."

The screen shifted to a vibrant image of diverse employees working together harmoniously. "Fourth, let's build **strong relationships**. Confucianism teaches us the importance of respect and harmony in relationships. Foster a culture of mutual respect. Encourage mentorship and teamwork. Recognize and celebrate the strengths and contributions of each individual."

Michael looked around, seeing the ideas taking root in the minds of his executives. "Finally," he said, "commit to **continuous learning**. Philosophy is about the pursuit of knowledge. Encourage your teams to read, learn, and grow. Host regular knowledge-sharing sessions where employees can discuss new ideas, books, or articles they've encountered. Promote an environment where curiosity and intellectual growth are valued."

He turned off the projector and stepped back to the center of the room, bringing the discussion full circle. "Applying these philosophical concepts is not about adding extra tasks to our already busy schedules. It's about infusing our daily practices with deeper meaning and purpose. It's about transforming our approach to management so that every action, decision, and interaction reflects our commitment to wisdom, integrity, and human flourishing."

Michael's eyes met those of his team, each person now seeing the path ahead not just as a series of steps, but as a journey toward becoming better leaders and individuals.

"Together," he concluded, "we can create a workplace that not only achieves outstanding results but also stands as a beacon of ethical leadership and human dignity. Let's take these philosophical principles and make them the cornerstone of our management practices."

The room was filled with a renewed sense of purpose and determination. The executives were ready to take the insights of philosophy and turn them into practical actions that would reshape their organization, infusing it with wisdom and integrity at every level.

Chapter 2: Ethics in Management

The Role of Ethics in Business Decisions

The morning sun streamed through the glass walls of the conference room at Apex Global Consulting, casting a warm glow on the polished table. Michael stood at the head of the table, his presence calm yet commanding, ready to delve into the next critical aspect of their journey: ethics in management.

"Good morning, everyone," Michael began, his voice resonating with the gravity of the topic. "Today, we explore the role of ethics in business decisions. Ethics is not just a set of rules—it's the foundation of trust, integrity, and sustainability in our organization."

He glanced around the room, meeting the eyes of his team members, ensuring they were ready to engage deeply with the subject.

"Let's start with a scenario," Michael proposed, clicking a button to reveal a slide depicting a bustling urban neighborhood. "Imagine our company is considering opening a new manufacturing plant. The site is ideal in many ways—cost-effective, strategic location, and ample resources. But there's a catch: the local community is concerned about potential environmental and social impacts."

The executives leaned forward, intrigued by the practical application of ethics Michael was about to present.

"In making this decision," Michael continued, "we face a classic ethical dilemma. On one hand, the plant promises significant economic benefits—jobs, increased production capacity, and higher profits. On the other hand, we must consider the potential harm to the community and the environment."

He paused, letting the weight of the dilemma sink in. "This is where ethical frameworks come into play. Let's examine three key ethical theories to guide our decision."

Michael clicked to the next slide, which featured a balance scale. "First, we have **Utilitarianism**. This approach asks us to consider the consequences of our actions and choose the option that maximizes overall happiness and minimizes harm. So, we need to weigh the economic benefits against the potential environmental and social costs. Can we find ways to mitigate the negative impacts? Perhaps invest in green technologies or community development programs?"

The team nodded, understanding the balance they must strike.

"Next," Michael continued, shifting to a slide with a compass pointing north, "is **Deontological Ethics**, championed by Immanuel Kant. This theory focuses on the morality of actions based on adherence to rules and duties, regardless of the outcome. Here, our duty might be to uphold principles like honesty, fairness, and respect for human rights. We must ask ourselves: Are we respecting the community's concerns? Are we transparent about our intentions and processes?"

He saw the team members reflect on their responsibilities as stewards of ethical behavior within the organization.

"Lastly," Michael said, the slide changing to a picture of Aristotle, "we consider **Virtue Ethics**. This approach emphasizes the character and virtues of the decision-makers. It's about asking, 'What kind of company do we want to be?' Do we want to be known for our integrity, compassion, and commitment to the common good? This perspective encourages us to act in ways that build trust and respect in the long term."

Michael turned off the projector and moved closer to the table, making the discussion more intimate. "By applying these ethical frameworks, we can navigate complex decisions with greater clarity and moral conviction. It's not just about making the right choice in a single instance but about embedding ethical thinking into our organizational DNA."

He looked at his team, each person contemplating the profound implications of ethics in their daily decisions. "Remember," Michael said, "ethical management isn't about perfection. It's about striving for integrity and making thoughtful, principled choices. It's about being accountable and transparent, even when it's difficult."

Michael's voice softened, but his words carried deep significance. "The role of ethics in business decisions is paramount. It's what builds trust with our stakeholders, sustains our reputation, and ensures our long-term success. As leaders, it's our duty to model ethical behavior and create a culture where ethical considerations are integral to every decision we make."

The room was silent, filled with a sense of resolve and responsibility. The executives understood that their choices went beyond profits and performance metrics; they were about shaping the ethical foundation of their company.

With newfound determination, the team prepared to integrate these ethical principles into their strategic discussions, ready to lead with integrity and wisdom. The path ahead was clear: ethical management was not just a practice but a commitment to a higher standard of leadership, one that would guide Apex Global Consulting toward a future defined by trust, respect, and enduring success.

Major Ethical Theories (Utilitarianism, Deontology, Virtue Ethics)

The room was charged with a sense of purpose as Michael prepared to delve deeper into the ethical theories that would guide their decision-making. The team at Apex Global Consulting sat attentively, ready to explore the philosophical foundations of ethics in business.

"Let's take a closer look at the major ethical theories that we've touched upon," Michael said, his tone both serious and engaging. "Understanding these theories will provide us with the tools to navigate our ethical dilemmas with confidence and clarity."

He clicked the remote, and the screen displayed a bustling cityscape, symbolizing the dynamic and interconnected world of business.

"First, let's examine **Utilitarianism**," Michael began. "Developed by Jeremy Bentham and John Stuart Mill, this theory is all about outcomes. The fundamental principle here is to maximize overall happiness and minimize suffering."

The slide transitioned to an image of a balance scale, highlighting the concept of weighing consequences. "Imagine we're deciding whether to launch a new product. A utilitarian approach would have us consider the potential benefits and harms of this decision. Will it improve the lives of our customers? Will it create jobs and economic growth? Or will it cause environmental damage or harm to local communities?"

He looked around the room, seeing the team members nodding thoughtfully. "Utilitarianism encourages us to think broadly about the impact of our actions and strive for the greatest good for the greatest number. It's a powerful tool for evaluating our choices, but it requires us to carefully consider and balance all potential consequences."

Michael clicked to the next slide, which featured an image of Immanuel Kant and a set of scales tipped toward principles. "Next, we have **Deontology**, rooted in the work of Immanuel Kant. Unlike utilitarianism, deontology is focused on duties and principles rather than outcomes. It's about doing the right thing because it's inherently the right thing to do."

The screen displayed a series of ethical maxims, each representing a fundamental duty. "According to Kant, we should act according to maxims that we would want to become universal laws. For instance, if honesty is a principle we value, then we must be honest in all our dealings, regardless of the consequences."

He saw the team members considering this rigorous standard. "Deontology requires us to adhere to our ethical principles consistently. It's about upholding our moral duties, such as honesty, fairness, and respect, even when it's challenging. This approach provides a strong ethical foundation but can sometimes be rigid, as it doesn't always account for complex, real-world scenarios."

Michael moved to the next slide, which showed a classical

image of Aristotle teaching his disciples. "Finally, let's explore **Virtue Ethics**, which traces back to Aristotle. This theory emphasizes the development of virtuous character traits, such as courage, wisdom, and compassion."

The slide displayed a series of virtues, each illustrated with a corresponding business scenario. "Virtue ethics asks us to consider the kind of people we want to be and the kind of organization we want to create. It's about cultivating habits and behaviors that reflect our highest values."

He looked at his team, the concepts clearly resonating with them. "For example, if we value integrity, we should foster a culture where integrity is practiced and celebrated. Virtue ethics is about long-term character building. It's less about specific actions and more about the overall moral character we develop and demonstrate through our actions."

Michael turned off the projector and returned to the center of the room, where he felt most connected with his team. "These three ethical theories—utilitarianism, deontology, and virtue ethics—each offer unique perspectives and tools for ethical decision-making. By understanding and integrating these theories, we can navigate the complexities of our business environment with greater moral clarity and purpose."

He paused, allowing his words to settle in. "In practice, this means considering the outcomes of our actions, adhering to our moral duties, and striving to develop virtuous character traits. It's about creating a balanced approach to ethics that reflects our commitment to integrity and excellence."

The team members exchanged thoughtful glances, the depth of the discussion clearly impacting their understanding of ethical leadership.

"Remember," Michael concluded, his voice steady and

inspiring, "ethics is not just a theoretical exercise. It's a practical guide for our daily decisions and actions. As we move forward, let's commit to applying these ethical principles in all aspects of our work, ensuring that our actions reflect the highest standards of integrity and respect."

The room was filled with a renewed sense of commitment and determination. The executives of Apex Global Consulting were ready to embrace these ethical theories, integrating them into their management practices to build a company grounded in moral excellence and guided by wisdom.

With a clear vision and a shared understanding of their ethical responsibilities, the team prepared to lead with integrity, setting a new standard for ethical leadership in the business world.

Case Studies of Ethical Dilemmas in Management

The energy in the room was palpable as Michael transitioned into the next segment of their discussion. The executives at Apex Global Consulting were ready to see how the ethical theories they had explored could be applied to real-world scenarios.

"To truly understand the application of these ethical principles," Michael said, "we need to look at case studies of ethical dilemmas in management. These examples will show us how to navigate complex situations with integrity and moral clarity."

He clicked the remote, and the screen displayed a headline: **"The Dilemma of Outsourcing."**

"Let's start with a familiar issue: outsourcing," Michael began. "Our company is considering outsourcing production to a country where labor costs are significantly lower. The financial benefits are clear—reduced costs and increased profitability. But what about the ethical implications?"

The slide changed to show a bustling factory in a developing country. "The potential issues include poor working conditions, low wages, and the impact on our current employees who might lose their jobs. How do we approach this dilemma?"

Michael gestured towards the screen. "Using **Utilitarianism**, we would evaluate the overall happiness and harm. We might ask: Does the economic benefit for our company and customers outweigh the potential harm to workers abroad and our displaced employees? Can we find ways to ensure fair wages and safe working conditions in the outsourced location?"

He clicked to the next slide, which displayed an image of an executive signing a contract. "From a **Deontological** perspective, we would consider our duties and principles. Do we have a duty to our current employees to ensure their job security? Do we have a moral obligation to ensure ethical labor practices, regardless of the financial benefits?"

Michael paused, letting the team reflect on these questions. "And from a **Virtue Ethics** standpoint, we consider the virtues we want to embody as a company. Do we value compassion, fairness, and responsibility? How can we demonstrate these virtues in our decision-making process?"

The screen transitioned to the next case study: **"Environmental Responsibility and Corporate Profit."**

"Another common dilemma involves environmental responsibility," Michael continued. "Imagine we have the opportunity to invest in a highly profitable project that, unfortunately, has significant environmental impacts. The project promises substantial returns, but it also risks considerable harm to local ecosystems."

The slide displayed a pristine natural landscape threatened by industrial development. "A **Utilitarian** approach would require us to weigh the economic benefits against the environmental damage. Is there a way to minimize the harm? Can we invest in technologies or initiatives that mitigate the environmental impact?"

He moved to the next slide showing a legal document. "From a **Deontological** perspective, we must ask: Do we have a duty to protect the environment? Are we adhering to ethical principles of sustainability and stewardship, regardless of the potential profits?"

Michael glanced around the room, ensuring everyone was engaged. "And with **Virtue Ethics**, we consider our character and the legacy we want to leave. Do we want to be known as a company that prioritizes profits over the planet? Or do we aspire to be leaders in sustainability and ethical responsibility?"

The final case study appeared on the screen: **"Whistleblowing in the Workplace."**

"Let's consider the scenario of whistleblowing," Michael said. "An employee discovers that a senior executive is involved in unethical practices, such as financial misconduct or discrimination. Reporting this could jeopardize the employee's career and disrupt the company, but remaining silent allows the unethical behavior to continue."

The slide displayed a silhouette of a lone whistleblower. "From a **Utilitarian** perspective, we need to consider the greater good. Does exposing the wrongdoing prevent further harm and promote justice, even at a personal or organizational cost?"

He clicked to the next slide, showing an ethical code of conduct. "In terms of **Deontological Ethics**, we must ask: Do we have a duty to uphold transparency and accountability? Is there a moral obligation to report unethical behavior, regardless of the consequences?"

The final slide showed a team united in trust. "And from a **Virtue Ethics** viewpoint, we reflect on the virtues of courage and integrity. Do we want to foster a culture where ethical behavior is paramount and individuals feel empowered to speak up against wrongdoing?"

Michael turned off the projector, bringing the room back to a more intimate setting. "These case studies illustrate the complexity of ethical dilemmas in management. By applying Utilitarianism, Deontology, and Virtue Ethics, we can navigate these challenges thoughtfully and ethically."

He looked at each team member, their faces reflecting deep contemplation and resolve. "Ethical dilemmas require us to balance multiple perspectives and values. Our goal is to make decisions that not only benefit our company but also uphold our moral integrity and contribute positively to society."

The room was filled with a renewed sense of purpose. The executives at Apex Global Consulting were ready to face their ethical challenges head-on, guided by the principles and wisdom they had explored.

With clear examples and a robust ethical framework, the team prepared to integrate these lessons into their daily practices, ensuring that every decision they made would be a testament to their commitment to ethical leadership and responsible management.

Developing an Ethical Framework for Leadership

The atmosphere in the conference room was charged with a blend of reflection and determination. Michael had guided the team through the exploration of ethical theories and their application to real-world dilemmas. Now, it was time to bring these insights together to create a concrete, actionable ethical framework for leadership at Apex Global Consulting.

"All right, team," Michael began, his voice steady and purposeful. "We've explored the theories and examined case studies. Now, it's time to develop our own ethical framework for leadership. This framework will serve as our guiding star, helping us navigate complex decisions with integrity and moral clarity."

He clicked the remote, and the screen displayed the title: **"Developing an Ethical Framework for Leadership."**

"First," Michael said, "we need to establish our **core values**. These are the fundamental principles that will guide all our actions and decisions. Let's brainstorm—what are the values we hold most dear as a company?"

The executives began to speak up, their voices overlapping with enthusiasm.

"Integrity," said Sarah, the CFO. "Without integrity, nothing else matters."

"Respect," added James, head of HR. "For our employees, our customers, and our community."

"Innovation," suggested Lisa, the CTO. "We must be forward-thinking, but in an ethical manner."

"Excellence," Michael nodded, adding another value. "Striving for the highest standards in everything we do."

As they settled on these core values, Michael typed them into the framework on the screen. "Integrity, Respect, Innovation, Excellence. These will be the pillars of our ethical framework."

He clicked to the next slide, which displayed a compass. "Next, we need to define **guiding principles** based on these values. These principles will help us apply our core values in practical ways. For example, under Integrity, we could have principles like 'Always act honestly,' 'Ensure transparency in all dealings,' and 'Hold ourselves accountable.'"

The room buzzed with activity as the team worked together to articulate principles for each value. After some discussion, they settled on the following:

Integrity:

- Always act honestly.
- Ensure transparency in all dealings.
- Hold ourselves accountable.

Respect:

- Treat everyone with dignity and fairness.
- Listen actively and empathetically.
- Foster an inclusive and diverse environment.

Innovation:

- Encourage creativity and forward-thinking.
- Consider the ethical implications of new technologies.
- Balance risk-taking with responsible practices.

Excellence:

- Strive for the highest standards in all we do.
- Continuously improve and learn.
- Deliver exceptional value to our stakeholders.

Michael captured these principles on the screen, creating a clear and structured framework. "These guiding principles will help us translate our core values into everyday actions."

He clicked to the next slide, which showed a scale balancing different elements. "Now, let's discuss **decision-making processes**. How do we ensure that our decisions align with our ethical framework?"

He looked around the room, inviting input. Sarah raised her hand. "We should implement a **decision checklist** that we use for all major decisions. It should include questions like, 'Does this decision uphold our core values?' 'Have we considered the potential impacts on all stakeholders?' and 'Are we being transparent and accountable?'"

"Great idea," Michael said, typing it into the framework. "We should also have a **review process** where decisions are evaluated by a diverse group of leaders to ensure different perspectives are considered."

James added, "And let's establish a **whistleblowing policy** to protect and empower those who report unethical behavior. It should ensure confidentiality and protection from retaliation."

Michael nodded, incorporating the suggestions. "Excellent. A decision checklist, a review process, and a whistleblowing policy will help us make ethical decisions consistently."

The screen transitioned to an image of people collaborating harmoniously. "Finally, let's talk about **embedding this framework into our culture**. It's not enough to have it on paper—we need to live it every day."

Lisa suggested, "We should provide **ongoing training** for all employees, focusing on our ethical framework and how to apply it in their roles."

James added, "And we should recognize and reward **ethical behavior**. Celebrate employees who exemplify our values and principles."

Michael agreed, "Let's also ensure **leadership accountability**. Our leaders must model these behaviors and be held accountable for upholding our ethical standards."

He added these elements to the framework: ongoing training, recognition and rewards, and leadership accountability.

Michael turned off the projector and faced his team, the room now buzzing with a shared sense of purpose. "We've developed a comprehensive ethical framework for leadership. This framework is our commitment to act with integrity, respect, innovation, and excellence in all we do."

He paused, letting the weight of their collective effort sink in. "By integrating these values and principles into our daily actions and decisions, we can lead with moral clarity and build a culture of ethical excellence. This is not just a framework—it's a promise we make to ourselves, our colleagues, and our stakeholders."

The team looked at Michael with renewed determination and solidarity. They were ready to take this framework and bring it to life, ensuring that every decision they made would reflect their deepest values and highest aspirations.

With this ethical framework as their guide, Apex Global Consulting was poised to set a new standard for ethical leadership, creating a workplace where integrity, respect, innovation, and excellence were not just ideals but lived realities.

The Impact of Ethical Management on Organizational Culture

The conference room at Apex Global Consulting was alive with a newfound energy. Michael had just walked the team through the creation of their ethical framework for leadership. Now, it was time to explore the broader impact of ethical management on their organizational culture.

"Thank you all for your input," Michael began, his voice resonating with enthusiasm. "We've developed a strong ethical framework. Now, let's discuss how ethical management influences our organizational culture."

He clicked the remote, and the screen displayed the title: **"The Impact of Ethical Management on Organizational Culture."**

"To start, consider this: an organization's culture is like the air we breathe—it's everywhere and affects everything we do," Michael said, gesturing to an image of a thriving, vibrant workplace. "When we lead with ethics, we create an environment where trust, respect, and collaboration can flourish."

He turned to the team, his eyes reflecting his conviction. "Let's explore how ethical management can transform our culture."

The screen shifted to a collage of diverse employees working together harmoniously. "First, ethical management builds **trust**," Michael explained. "When leaders act with integrity, employees feel secure and confident in their leadership. This trust encourages open communication and transparency."

He paused to let the significance of trust settle in. "Imagine a scenario where an employee faces a challenging situation but knows they can approach their manager without fear of judgment or retaliation. This openness not only resolves issues more effectively but also strengthens the bond between team members."

Sarah, the CFO, nodded. "I've seen how transparency in financial decisions has fostered a sense of trust and collaboration in my department. It makes a huge difference."

"Exactly," Michael agreed, clicking to the next slide, which showed employees engaging in a lively brainstorming session. "Second, ethical management promotes **innovation**. When employees feel respected and valued, they're more likely to take risks and think creatively."

He leaned forward, emphasizing his point. "In an ethical workplace, people know that their contributions are valued and that failures are seen as learning opportunities rather than occasions for blame. This fosters a culture of continuous improvement and innovation."

James, head of HR, interjected, "I've noticed that our most innovative ideas often come from those who feel most empowered and respected in the company. It's a direct correlation."

The next slide featured an image of a diverse team celebrating a milestone. "Third, ethical management enhances **diversity and inclusion**," Michael continued. "When we commit to fairness and respect, we create a welcoming environment for everyone, regardless of their background."

He saw Lisa, the CTO, nodding in agreement. "By embracing diverse perspectives, we not only become more inclusive but also more competitive. Different viewpoints lead to better problem-solving and innovation."

Michael smiled. "And when employees see that their company genuinely values diversity, they are more likely to be engaged and loyal. This reduces turnover and fosters a sense of belonging."

The screen transitioned to a group of employees collaborating on a project with evident enthusiasm. "Fourth, ethical management leads to **higher employee engagement and satisfaction**. When employees see that their leaders are committed to ethical practices, they feel proud to be part of the organization."

He looked around the room, seeing nods of agreement. "Engaged employees are more productive, motivated, and committed to the company's success. They take ownership of their work and go the extra mile, knowing they are part of something meaningful."

James added, "I've seen a marked improvement in morale and productivity since we started emphasizing our ethical values. It creates a positive feedback loop."

Michael clicked to the next slide, which showed a graph of company growth. "Finally, ethical management positively impacts our **reputation and long-term success**. Customers, partners, and investors are more likely to trust and support a company known for its integrity and ethical practices."

He turned to his team, his voice filled with conviction. "A strong ethical reputation attracts top talent, loyal customers, and reliable partners. It creates a sustainable foundation for growth and success."

Michael turned off the projector, bringing the focus back to the team. "In summary, ethical management transforms our organizational culture by building trust, promoting innovation, enhancing diversity and inclusion, increasing employee engagement, and boosting our reputation."

He paused, letting his words resonate. "This transformation doesn't happen overnight, but with consistent commitment and effort, we can create a culture where ethical practices are the norm and where every employee feels valued and empowered."

The room was filled with a sense of purpose and excitement. The executives at Apex Global Consulting were ready to lead by example, knowing that their commitment to ethical management would create a positive and lasting impact on their organizational culture.

"Let's take this framework and these insights," Michael concluded, "and make them a living part of our everyday actions and decisions. Together, we can build a company where ethical leadership is not just an aspiration but a reality—one that inspires and uplifts everyone who is part of our journey."

With a renewed sense of determination and unity, the team prepared to embed these ethical principles into the fabric of their company, transforming Apex Global Consulting into a beacon of ethical excellence and a model for others to follow.

Tools for Ethical Decision-Making

As the discussion continued, Michael turned the team's attention to the practical aspect of ethical management: tools for ethical decision-making.

"Ethical decision-making is not always straightforward," Michael began, his tone measured and purposeful. "That's why it's crucial to have tools and frameworks in place to guide us through the process."

He clicked the remote, and the screen displayed the title: **"Tools for Ethical Decision-Making."**

"Let's start with the **ethical decision-making framework**," Michael said, as he brought up a diagram illustrating the steps. "This framework provides a structured approach to evaluating ethical dilemmas."

He pointed to each step as he explained. "First, identify the problem or dilemma. Next, gather relevant information and consider different perspectives. Then, evaluate the situation using ethical principles and values. Generate options for action and consider the potential consequences. Finally, make a decision and take action, while monitoring and reflecting on the outcomes."

The team nodded, recognizing the importance of a systematic approach to ethical decision-making.

"Next," Michael continued, clicking to the next slide, "let's talk about **ethical decision-making models**. These models provide specific strategies for analyzing and resolving ethical dilemmas."

He displayed a list of popular models, including the ethical principles approach, the ethical tests approach, and the ethical decision-making grid. "Each model offers a different perspective and set of criteria for evaluating ethical choices. By familiarizing ourselves with these models, we can choose the one that best fits the situation at hand."

The executives leaned in, absorbing the information, eager to apply these models to their own decision-making processes.

"Now, let's discuss **ethical leadership assessment tools**," Michael said, moving to the next slide. "These tools help leaders assess their ethical behavior and identify areas for improvement."

He displayed examples of assessment tools, such as surveys, self-assessments, and 360-degree feedback. "By regularly assessing our ethical leadership practices, we can ensure that we are aligning our actions with our values and principles."

The team took notes, recognizing the value of ongoing self-reflection and improvement in ethical leadership.

"Lastly," Michael said, clicking to the final slide, "let's not forget about **training and development**. Providing training on ethical decision-making and leadership can equip our employees with the knowledge and skills they need to navigate ethical challenges effectively."

He highlighted the importance of interactive workshops, case studies, and role-playing exercises in enhancing ethical competence. "By investing in our employees' ethical literacy, we empower them to make ethical decisions with confidence and integrity."

The executives nodded in agreement, realizing the significance of investing in their team's ethical development.

"In summary," Michael concluded, "by leveraging these tools and resources, we can strengthen our ethical decision-making capabilities and foster a culture of integrity and accountability within our organization."

He turned off the projector and faced his team, a sense of determination evident in his gaze. "Let's commit to using these tools to guide our actions and decisions, ensuring that ethics remain at the forefront of everything we do."

The room was filled with a renewed sense of purpose and resolve. The executives of Apex Global Consulting were ready to embrace these tools and integrate them into their daily practices, knowing that they would help them navigate ethical challenges with clarity and confidence.

With these tools as their compass, they prepared to lead with integrity and uphold the highest ethical standards, setting a shining example for their organization and the business world at large.

Chapter 3: The Philosophy of Leadership

Defining Leadership from a Philosophical Perspective

The conference room at Apex Global Consulting was bathed in soft light, creating an atmosphere of introspection and anticipation. Michael, standing at the front of the room, was about to embark on a journey into the philosophical depths of leadership.

"Welcome, everyone, to Chapter 3 of our exploration: The Philosophy of Leadership," Michael began, his voice resonating with authority and curiosity. "Today, we dive into the essence of leadership from a philosophical perspective."

He clicked the remote, and the screen displayed the title: **"Defining Leadership from a Philosophical Perspective."**

"Leadership," Michael began, his eyes scanning the attentive faces of his team, "is a concept as old as civilization itself. But what does it truly mean to lead? How do we define leadership from a philosophical standpoint?"

He paused, allowing the questions to hang in the air, inviting the team to ponder their significance.

"At its core," Michael continued, "leadership is about influence. It's about inspiring others to achieve a common goal, to transcend their individual limitations, and to contribute to something greater than themselves."

The screen transitioned to a quote by Lao Tzu: "A leader is best when people barely know he exists. When his work is done, his aim fulfilled, they will say: we did it ourselves."

"Lao Tzu's words capture a fundamental truth about leadership," Michael explained. "True leadership is not about exerting control or authority but about empowering others to realize their potential. It's about creating a shared vision and fostering an environment where everyone feels valued and capable of contributing."

He clicked to the next slide, which displayed a series of questions: "What qualities make a great leader? Is leadership innate or learned? Can anyone be a leader?"

"These questions," Michael said, "have been debated by philosophers for centuries. And while there is no definitive answer, philosophers have offered valuable insights into the nature of leadership."

The screen shifted to a series of historical figures, from Socrates to Machiavelli to Martin Luther King Jr. "From Socrates, who emphasized the importance of self-awareness and introspection, to Machiavelli, who explored the pragmatic realities of power and authority, to Martin Luther King Jr., who inspired a nation with his vision of justice and equality, philosophers have provided us with diverse perspectives on leadership."

He paused, letting the significance of these figures sink in. "At its essence, leadership is a deeply human endeavor—a blend of character, vision, and action. It's about embodying values such as integrity, empathy, courage, and resilience."

The screen transitioned to a quote by Aristotle: "He who cannot be a good follower cannot be a good leader."

"Aristotle's words remind us that leadership is not just about leading from the front but also about serving and supporting those around us," Michael said. "It's about recognizing the importance of followership and understanding that true leadership emerges from a foundation of trust, respect, and collaboration."

He clicked to the final slide, which displayed a panoramic view of a mountain peak bathed in golden light. "In conclusion, leadership is a multifaceted concept that defies easy definition. It is shaped by our values, our experiences, and our interactions with others. But at its heart, leadership is about inspiring, guiding, and empowering others to reach new heights of achievement and fulfillment."

Michael turned off the projector and faced his team, a sense of reverence in his expression. "As we embark on this exploration of leadership from a philosophical perspective, let us remember that leadership is not just a role or a title—it's a way of being, a way of relating to others, and a profound opportunity to make a positive impact on the world."

The room was filled with a quiet reverence as the executives absorbed the wisdom of Michael's words. They understood that leadership was not just about authority or control but about service, inspiration, and empowerment.

With a renewed sense of purpose, they prepared to delve deeper into the philosophy of leadership, eager to uncover new insights and perspectives that would guide them on their journey to becoming truly exceptional leaders.

Classical and Modern Philosophical Views on Leadership

The room fell into a hushed reverence as Michael delved deeper into the philosophical underpinnings of leadership. The executives at Apex Global Consulting leaned forward, eager to explore the rich tapestry of classical and modern perspectives on this timeless concept.

"Let us now journey through the annals of philosophy," Michael began, his voice carrying a sense of reverence for the wisdom of the ages. "From the ancient Greeks to contemporary thinkers, philosophers have offered profound insights into the nature of leadership."

He clicked the remote, and the screen displayed the title: **"Classical and Modern Philosophical Views on Leadership."**

"First, let us turn our gaze to the wisdom of antiquity," Michael said, as he brought up an image of Plato and Aristotle engaging in deep discussion. "In the works of Plato and Aristotle, we find foundational ideas about the virtues of leadership."

He gestured to the screen. "Plato's concept of the philosopher-king emphasizes the importance of wisdom, justice, and moral integrity in leadership. According to Plato, the ideal leader is one who possesses not only knowledge and intellect but also a deep understanding of ethical principles."

The screen transitioned to an image of Aristotle's "Nicomachean Ethics." "Aristotle, on the other hand, focuses on the moral virtues that are essential for effective leadership. He emphasizes the importance of virtues such as courage, temperance, and magnanimity in guiding individuals and communities towards the common good."

Michael paused, allowing the weight of these ancient insights to settle in. "From Plato and Aristotle, we learn that leadership is not just about power or authority but about embodying virtuous qualities that inspire trust and respect."

He clicked to the next slide, which displayed a collage of modern philosophers, from Friedrich Nietzsche to Jean-Paul Sartre to bell hooks. "Now, let us fast forward to the modern era, where philosophers continue to offer fresh perspectives on leadership."

"In the existentialist tradition," Michael continued, "thinkers like Friedrich Nietzsche and Jean-Paul Sartre challenge traditional notions of leadership by emphasizing individual autonomy and personal responsibility."

The screen transitioned to a quote by Nietzsche: "The individual has always had to struggle to keep from being overwhelmed by the tribe. If you try it, you will be lonely often, and sometimes frightened. But no price is too high to pay for the privilege of owning yourself."

"Nietzsche reminds us that true leadership begins with self-mastery and authenticity," Michael explained. "It's about daring to stand apart from the crowd, to embrace one's unique vision and values, even in the face of adversity."

He clicked to the next slide, which featured a quote by bell hooks: "The function of freedom is to free someone else."

"In the feminist tradition," Michael continued, "thinkers like bell hooks challenge us to reexamine power dynamics and hierarchies in leadership. According to hooks, true leadership is about empowering others, especially those who have been marginalized or oppressed."

The executives nodded, recognizing the importance of

inclusive and empowering leadership in today's diverse world.

"From the classical wisdom of Plato and Aristotle to the modern insights of Nietzsche and hooks," Michael concluded, "philosophers continue to illuminate the path to enlightened leadership. By drawing on these diverse perspectives, we can cultivate a deeper understanding of leadership and forge a path towards more ethical, inclusive, and impactful leadership practices."

With a sense of reverence for the wisdom they had just encountered, the executives at Apex Global Consulting prepared to integrate these philosophical insights into their own leadership journey, knowing that they held the key to unlocking new heights of excellence and integrity in their roles as leaders.

Ethical Leadership: Principles and Practices

As the exploration of leadership continued, Michael turned the focus towards ethical leadership—a beacon of integrity and virtue in the tumultuous seas of organizational dynamics. The executives at Apex Global Consulting leaned in, eager to uncover the principles and practices that would guide them towards ethical excellence.

"Ethical leadership," Michael began, his voice steady and resolute, "stands as a pillar of moral integrity and responsibility in the realm of leadership. It is the embodiment of values such as honesty, fairness, and empathy, guiding individuals and organizations towards the path of righteousness and accountability."

He clicked the remote, and the screen displayed the title: **"Ethical Leadership: Principles and Practices."**

"Let us first illuminate the foundational principles of ethical leadership," Michael continued, his gaze sweeping across the room. "At its core, ethical leadership is grounded in a commitment to truth, justice, and the common good. It is about doing what is right, even when it is not easy or popular."

The screen transitioned to a quote by Mahatma Gandhi: "Be the change that you wish to see in the world."

"Gandhi's words encapsulate the essence of ethical leadership," Michael explained. "It is about leading by example, embodying the values and principles we wish to see reflected in the world around us."

He clicked to the next slide, which displayed a series of guiding principles: integrity, accountability, empathy, and courage. "These principles serve as the bedrock of ethical leadership, guiding our actions and decisions in alignment with our values and the greater good."

The executives nodded in agreement, recognizing the importance of these principles in guiding their leadership journey.

"Now, let us turn our attention to the practices of ethical leadership," Michael said, as he brought up an image of a leader listening attentively to their team. "Ethical leadership is not just about espousing lofty ideals—it is about translating those ideals into action through tangible behaviors and practices."

He gestured to the screen. "One of the key practices of ethical leadership is **transparency**. Transparent leaders communicate openly and honestly with their team, fostering an environment of trust and accountability."

The screen transitioned to an image of a leader taking responsibility for their actions. "Another crucial practice is **accountability**. Ethical leaders hold themselves and others accountable for their actions, taking ownership of their mistakes and learning from them."

Michael continued, "Empathy is also a hallmark of ethical leadership. Leaders who practice empathy seek to understand the perspectives and experiences of others, fostering a culture of compassion and inclusivity."

The screen shifted to a quote by Maya Angelou: "I've learned that people will forget what you said, people will forget what you did, but people will never forget how you made them feel."

"Finally," Michael said, "ethical leadership requires **courage**. It takes courage to stand up for what is right, to challenge the status quo, and to make difficult decisions in the face of adversity."

He paused, allowing the weight of these practices to sink in. "By embodying these principles and practices, we can cultivate a culture of ethical leadership within our organization—a culture where integrity, accountability, empathy, and courage are not just ideals but lived realities."

With a renewed sense of purpose and determination, the executives at Apex Global Consulting prepared to embrace ethical leadership as their guiding compass, knowing that it would lead them towards a brighter future filled with integrity, trust, and excellence.

The Role of Wisdom in Leadership

As the discussion on leadership unfolded, Michael steered the conversation towards a profound aspect often overlooked in the realm of leadership: wisdom. The executives at Apex Global Consulting listened intently, eager to understand the transformative role wisdom played in guiding leaders towards enlightened decision-making and actions.

"Let us now delve into the essence of wisdom in leadership," Michael began, his voice infused with a sense of reverence for the profound insights that awaited exploration. "Wisdom transcends mere knowledge and expertise—it is the culmination of experience, reflection, and discernment, guiding leaders towards paths of virtue and enlightenment."

He clicked the remote, and the screen displayed the title: **"The Role of Wisdom in Leadership."**

"Wisdom," Michael continued, "is the compass that guides leaders through the complexities and uncertainties of the modern world. It is the ability to discern truth from falsehood, to navigate ethical dilemmas with clarity and integrity, and to inspire others towards the highest ideals of human flourishing."

The screen transitioned to a quote by Confucius: "By three methods we may learn wisdom: First, by reflection, which is noblest; Second, by imitation, which is easiest; and third by experience, which is the bitterest."

"Confucius reminds us that wisdom is not acquired through mere accumulation of knowledge or credentials," Michael explained. "It is cultivated through deep reflection on our experiences, through observing the actions of wise leaders, and through the crucible of lived experience."

He clicked to the next slide, which displayed a series of qualities associated with wise leadership: humility, empathy, discernment, and resilience. "Wise leaders embody these qualities, serving as beacons of inspiration and guidance for those around them."

The executives nodded in agreement, recognizing the profound impact wise leadership could have on individuals and organizations.

CHAPTER 3: THE PHILOSOPHY OF LEADERSHIP

"Now, let us explore the practices of wise leadership," Michael said, as he brought up an image of a leader seeking counsel from their team. "One of the key practices of wise leadership is **humility**. Wise leaders acknowledge their limitations and seek input and advice from others, recognizing that true wisdom lies in collaboration and collective insight."

The screen transitioned to an image of a leader empathizing with their team members. "Empathy is another hallmark of wise leadership. Wise leaders seek to understand the perspectives and experiences of others, fostering a culture of compassion and inclusivity."

Michael continued, "Discernment is also essential for wise leadership. Wise leaders possess the ability to discern truth from falsehood, to make sound judgments in the face of uncertainty, and to navigate complex ethical dilemmas with clarity and integrity."

The screen shifted to a quote by Winston Churchill: "Courage is what it takes to stand up and speak; courage is also what it takes to sit down and listen."

"Finally," Michael said, "wise leadership requires resilience. Wise leaders persevere in the face of adversity, learning from setbacks and challenges, and emerging stronger and wiser from the experience."

He paused, allowing the significance of these practices to sink in. "By embodying these qualities and practices, we can cultivate a culture of wise leadership within our organization—a culture where humility, empathy, discernment, and resilience are not just ideals but lived realities."

With a renewed sense of reverence for the transformative power of wisdom, the executives at Apex Global Consulting prepared to integrate these insights into their leadership journey, knowing that they held the key to unlocking new levels of excellence, integrity, and impact in their roles as leaders.

Case Studies of Philosophical Leadership

As the discussion on leadership continued to unfold, Michael shifted the focus towards the examination of real-world examples where philosophical principles were embodied in leadership practices. The executives at Apex Global Consulting leaned forward, eager to dissect these case studies and glean insights that would shape their own leadership approach.

"Let us now turn our attention to case studies of philosophical leadership," Michael began, his voice tinged with anticipation for the profound lessons that awaited exploration. "These case studies offer us invaluable insights into how philosophical principles can be applied in real-world leadership scenarios, guiding individuals and organizations towards ethical excellence and impact."

He clicked the remote, and the screen displayed the title: **"Case Studies of Philosophical Leadership."**

"Our first case study," Michael began, "is that of Mahatma Gandhi—an icon of moral leadership and nonviolent resistance."

The screen transitioned to images of Gandhi leading the Indian independence movement. "Gandhi's leadership was grounded in the philosophy of ahimsa, or nonviolence. He believed that true strength lay not in the use of force or coercion, but in the power of love, truth, and compassion."

Michael continued, "Through his commitment to nonviolent protest and civil disobedience, Gandhi inspired millions to join him in the struggle for freedom and justice. His leadership serves as a timeless example of how philosophical principles can be translated into transformative action."

The executives nodded in admiration, recognizing the profound impact Gandhi's leadership had on shaping the course of history.

"Our next case study," Michael said, clicking to the next slide, "is that of Nelson Mandela—a visionary leader who embodied the principles of reconciliation and forgiveness."

The screen displayed images of Mandela's journey from political prisoner to South Africa's first black president. "Mandela's leadership was guided by the philosophy of ubuntu—a belief in the interconnectedness of all humanity and the importance of empathy, forgiveness, and reconciliation."

Michael continued, "Despite enduring 27 years of imprisonment, Mandela emerged with a spirit of forgiveness and a vision of reconciliation. His leadership in dismantling apartheid and fostering national unity serves as a powerful testament to the transformative power of philosophical principles in leadership."

The executives sat in contemplative silence, moved by Mandela's unwavering commitment to justice and reconciliation.

"Our final case study," Michael said, clicking to the last slide, "is that of Malala Yousafzai—a courageous advocate for girls' education and human rights."

The screen displayed images of Malala speaking out for girls' rights to education. "Malala's leadership is grounded in the philosophy of courage and resilience. Despite facing threats and violence from the Taliban, Malala refused to be silenced, continuing to speak out for the rights of girls to education and empowerment."

Michael continued, "Through her unwavering courage and commitment to her principles, Malala has inspired millions around the world to stand up for justice and equality. Her leadership demonstrates the transformative impact of philosophical principles in the face of adversity."

The executives sat in awe of Malala's bravery and resilience, inspired by her example of leadership in the pursuit of justice and equality.

"In conclusion," Michael said, turning off the projector and facing his team, "these case studies remind us that philosophical principles have the power to transform individuals and societies. By drawing inspiration from these examples, we can cultivate a deeper understanding of leadership and harness the transformative power of philosophy in our own leadership journey."

With a renewed sense of purpose and determination, the executives at Apex Global Consulting prepared to integrate the lessons learned from these case studies into their own leadership practices, knowing that they held the key to unlocking new levels of ethical excellence and impact in their roles as leaders.

Developing Leadership Philosophically

As the discussion on leadership continued to unfold, Michael turned the spotlight towards a pivotal aspect of leadership development: the philosophical approach. The executives at Apex Global Consulting leaned in, eager to explore how they could cultivate their leadership philosophically, unlocking new depths of wisdom and insight along their journey.

"Let us now embark on the exploration of developing

leadership philosophically," Michael began, his voice infused with a sense of purpose and introspection. "By embracing a philosophical approach to leadership development, we can cultivate a deeper understanding of ourselves, our values, and our purpose as leaders."

He clicked the remote, and the screen displayed the title: **"Developing Leadership Philosophically."**

"Our journey begins with **self-awareness**," Michael continued, gesturing to the screen. "Self-awareness is the foundation of philosophical leadership—it is the ability to introspectively examine our thoughts, emotions, and actions, gaining insight into our strengths, weaknesses, and values."

The screen transitioned to a quote by Socrates: "Know thyself."

"Socrates' timeless wisdom reminds us of the importance of self-awareness in leadership," Michael explained. "By engaging in practices such as journaling, meditation, and self-reflection, we can cultivate a deeper understanding of ourselves, uncovering the values and principles that guide our leadership journey."

The executives nodded in agreement, recognizing the transformative power of self-awareness in leadership development.

"Next," Michael said, clicking to the next slide, "let us explore the concept of **philosophical inquiry**. Philosophical inquiry is the process of questioning assumptions, exploring alternative perspectives, and seeking deeper understanding of complex issues."

The screen displayed images of a group engaged in lively discussion. "By engaging in philosophical inquiry, we can broaden our perspectives, challenge conventional wisdom, and foster critical thinking skills essential for effective leadership."

Michael continued, "Through practices such as Socratic dialogue, debate, and philosophical reading, we can cultivate a habit of inquiry, continuously seeking truth and wisdom in our leadership endeavors."

The executives leaned forward, eager to embrace the spirit of inquiry in their own leadership development.

"Our journey of developing leadership philosophically also involves **values clarification**," Michael said, bringing up an image of a compass. "Values clarification is the process of identifying and prioritizing our core values, aligning our actions and decisions with what truly matters to us."

The screen transitioned to a quote by Viktor Frankl: "Between stimulus and response there is a space. In that space is our power to choose our response. In our response lies our growth and our freedom."

"Frankl's words remind us that our values shape our choices and actions," Michael explained. "By clarifying our values and reflecting on how they inform our leadership approach, we can cultivate greater authenticity, integrity, and purpose in our leadership journey."

The executives nodded thoughtfully, recognizing the importance of values clarification in leadership development.

"In conclusion," Michael said, turning off the projector and facing his team, "developing leadership philosophically is a journey of self-discovery, inquiry, and values alignment. By embracing a philosophical approach to leadership development, we can cultivate a deeper understanding of ourselves and our role as leaders, unlocking new levels of wisdom, authenticity, and impact along the way."

With a renewed sense of purpose and determination, the

executives at Apex Global Consulting prepared to embark on their journey of developing leadership philosophically, knowing that it held the key to unlocking new heights of excellence and fulfillment in their roles as leaders.

Chapter 4: The Role of Purpose in Management

Philosophical Foundations of Organizational Purpose

In the heart of Apex Global Consulting's boardroom, Michael stood poised to delve into the profound exploration of purpose in management. With the executives eagerly anticipating his words, he embarked on a journey into the philosophical foundations that underpin organizational purpose.

"Welcome, everyone, to Chapter 4: The Role of Purpose in Management," Michael began, his voice carrying a blend of gravitas and anticipation. "Today, we explore the philosophical underpinnings that shape and define the purpose of organizations—a journey that transcends mere profit and ventures into the realm of meaning and significance."

He clicked the remote, and the screen displayed the title: **"Philosophical Foundations of Organizational Purpose."**

"At the core of every organization lies a deeper question: Why do we exist?" Michael posed, his gaze sweeping across the room. "This question delves beyond the pursuit of profit and success—it touches upon the fundamental essence of our existence, our values, and our impact on the world."

The screen transitioned to a quote by Aristotle: "Happiness is the meaning and the purpose of life, the whole aim and end of human existence."

"Aristotle's timeless wisdom reminds us that true fulfillment and purpose stem from aligning our actions with our values and contributing to the greater good," Michael explained. "This principle applies not only to individuals but also to organizations."

He clicked to the next slide, which displayed a series of philosophical perspectives on organizational purpose: utilitarianism, deontology, existentialism, and virtue ethics. "From utilitarianism's focus on maximizing the greatest good for the greatest number to deontology's emphasis on moral duty and obligation, philosophers offer diverse perspectives on the ethical foundations of organizational purpose."

The executives nodded, recognizing the significance of these philosophical perspectives in shaping organizational values and direction.

"Existentialism," Michael continued, "challenges us to confront the existential question of 'why'—to reflect on the deeper meaning and purpose of our existence as individuals and organizations. It encourages us to embrace our freedom and responsibility in shaping our own destiny."

The screen shifted to a quote by Jean-Paul Sartre: "We are our choices."

"Sartre's words remind us that organizational purpose is not predetermined—it is created through the choices and actions of individuals within the organization," Michael elaborated. "It is a reflection of our collective values, aspirations, and commitments."

He clicked to the final slide, which displayed a quote by Aristotle: "Where your talents and the needs of the world cross, there lies your vocation."

"In summary," Michael concluded, "the philosophical foundations of organizational purpose remind us that true fulfillment and success stem from aligning our actions with our values and contributing to the greater good. By embracing a purpose-driven approach to management, we can create organizations that are not only successful but also meaningful and impactful."

With a renewed sense of purpose and clarity, the executives at Apex Global Consulting prepared to embark on their journey of defining and shaping their organizational purpose, knowing that it held the key to unlocking new levels of fulfillment, significance, and impact in their work.

Defining and Articulating Purpose

As the discussion on organizational purpose continued, Michael shifted the focus towards the crucial task of defining and articulating purpose—a beacon that guides organizations towards their desired destination. The executives at Apex Global Consulting leaned in, eager to uncover the strategies and insights that would help them craft a compelling purpose for their organization.

"Let us now embark on the exploration of defining and articulating purpose," Michael began, his voice resonating with a blend of determination and introspection. "At the heart of every successful organization lies a clear and compelling purpose—a North Star that guides its actions, inspires its people, and drives its success."

He clicked the remote, and the screen displayed the title: **"Defining and Articulating Purpose."**

"Our journey begins with **clarity**," Michael continued, gesturing to the screen. "A clear and concise purpose statement is essential for aligning the efforts and energies of everyone within the organization towards a common goal."

The screen transitioned to a quote by Simon Sinek: "People don't buy what you do; they buy why you do it."

"Sinek's words remind us of the importance of articulating not just what we do, but why we do it," Michael explained. "A compelling purpose statement communicates the organization's values, aspirations, and impact, inspiring both employees and stakeholders alike."

The executives nodded in agreement, recognizing the power of a clear and compelling purpose statement in driving organizational success.

"Next," Michael said, clicking to the next slide, "let us explore the concept of **authenticity**. An authentic purpose resonates deeply with the values and identity of the organization, reflecting its unique strengths, passions, and aspirations."

The screen displayed images of organizations exemplifying authenticity in their purpose statements. "By staying true to who we are and what we stand for, we can create a purpose statement that is genuine, credible, and inspiring."

Michael continued, "An authentic purpose statement serves as a rallying cry for employees, a guiding light in times of uncertainty, and a powerful magnet for attracting like-minded customers, partners, and investors."

The executives leaned forward, eager to imbue their organization's purpose with authenticity and resonance.

"Our journey of defining and articulating purpose also

involves **engagement**," Michael said, bringing up an image of a team brainstorming session. "Engaging employees in the process of defining and articulating purpose fosters a sense of ownership, commitment, and alignment with the organization's goals and values."

The screen transitioned to a quote by Margaret Mead: "Never doubt that a small group of thoughtful, committed citizens can change the world; indeed, it's the only thing that ever has."

"By involving employees at all levels of the organization in the purpose-defining process," Michael explained, "we can tap into their diverse perspectives, insights, and ideas, creating a purpose statement that truly reflects the collective aspirations and values of the organization."

He paused, allowing the significance of these strategies to sink in. "In conclusion," Michael said, turning off the projector and facing his team, "defining and articulating purpose is not just a task—it is a journey of discovery, alignment, and inspiration. By embracing clarity, authenticity, and engagement, we can create a purpose statement that serves as a guiding light for our organization, igniting passion, driving innovation, and catalyzing success."

With a renewed sense of purpose and commitment, the executives at Apex Global Consulting prepared to embark on their journey of defining and articulating purpose, knowing that it held the key to unlocking new levels of alignment, engagement, and success in their organization.

CHAPTER 4: THE ROLE OF PURPOSE IN MANAGEMENT

Aligning Business Strategies with Organizational Purpose

As the discussion on organizational purpose continued, Michael turned the focus towards the critical task of aligning business strategies with this overarching mission—a pivotal step in driving the organization towards its desired destination. The executives at Apex Global Consulting leaned forward, eager to uncover the strategies and insights that would help them integrate purpose seamlessly into their business operations.

"Let us now explore the crucial process of aligning business strategies with organizational purpose," Michael began, his voice imbued with a sense of urgency and determination. "At the heart of every successful organization lies a strategic roadmap that is intricately woven with its purpose—a roadmap that guides its actions, decisions, and investments towards the fulfillment of its mission."

He clicked the remote, and the screen displayed the title: **"Aligning Business Strategies with Organizational Purpose."**

"Our journey begins with **clarity**," Michael continued, gesturing to the screen. "A clear understanding of the organization's purpose is essential for informing strategic decision-making and prioritizing initiatives that advance its mission."

The screen transitioned to a quote by Peter Drucker: "The purpose of business is to create and keep a customer."

"Drucker's words remind us that organizational purpose is not just a lofty ideal—it is the driving force behind every business decision and action," Michael explained. "By aligning business strategies with purpose, we can create value for our customers, stakeholders, and society at large, fostering sustainable growth and impact."

The executives nodded in agreement, recognizing the importance of clarity in aligning strategies with purpose.

"Next," Michael said, clicking to the next slide, "let us explore the concept of **integration**. Integrating purpose into every aspect of the organization's operations, from product development to marketing to employee engagement, ensures that purpose becomes embedded in its DNA."

The screen displayed images of organizations exemplifying integration of purpose into their business strategies. "By infusing purpose into the organization's culture, processes, and systems, we can create a cohesive and aligned approach to achieving our mission."

Michael continued, "An integrated approach to purpose ensures that every decision and action—from launching new products to engaging with stakeholders—is guided by the organization's values, aspirations, and impact goals."

The executives leaned forward, eager to integrate purpose seamlessly into their organization's strategies and operations.

"Our journey of aligning business strategies with organizational purpose also involves **measurement**," Michael said, bringing up an image of a dashboard displaying key performance indicators. "Measuring the impact of purpose-driven initiatives and tracking progress towards our mission goals allows us to assess the effectiveness of our strategies and make informed adjustments as needed."

The screen transitioned to a quote by Peter F. Drucker: "What gets measured gets managed."

"Drucker's words remind us of the importance of accountability and transparency in driving organizational performance," Michael explained. "By establishing clear metrics and benchmarks for measuring the impact of purpose-driven initiatives, we can ensure that our strategies are aligned with our mission and driving meaningful results."

He paused, allowing the significance of these strategies to sink in. "In conclusion," Michael said, turning off the projector and facing his team, "aligning business strategies with organizational purpose is not just a strategic imperative— it is a moral imperative. By embracing clarity, integration, and measurement, we can create a purpose-driven organization that is not only successful but also meaningful and impactful."

With a renewed sense of purpose and commitment, the executives at Apex Global Consulting prepared to integrate purpose seamlessly into their business strategies, knowing that it held the key to unlocking new levels of alignment, engagement, and impact in their organization.

Purpose-Driven Leadership

As the discussion on organizational purpose continued, Michael turned the spotlight towards the pivotal role of purpose-driven leadership—a beacon that guides individuals and organizations towards their highest aspirations and impact. The executives at Apex Global Consulting leaned in, eager to uncover the transformative power of purpose-driven leadership in driving organizational success.

"Let us now explore the profound impact of purpose-driven leadership," Michael began, his voice resonating with conviction and inspiration. "At the heart of every successful organization lies a purpose-driven leader—a visionary who inspires, empowers, and guides others towards the fulfillment of the organization's mission."

He clicked the remote, and the screen displayed the title: **"Purpose-Driven Leadership."**

"Our journey begins with **vision**," Michael continued, gesturing to the screen. "A purpose-driven leader is guided by a clear and compelling vision—a vision that articulates the organization's purpose, values, and aspirations, inspiring others to rally behind a shared cause."

The screen transitioned to a quote by John F. Kennedy: "Efforts and courage are not enough without purpose and direction."

"Kennedy's words remind us of the importance of vision in driving meaningful change and progress," Michael explained. "By casting a bold vision that is rooted in the organization's purpose, a purpose-driven leader ignites passion, fosters alignment, and mobilizes action towards a common goal."

The executives nodded in agreement, recognizing the transformative power of vision in purpose-driven leadership.

"Next," Michael said, clicking to the next slide, "let us explore the concept of **authenticity**. A purpose-driven leader leads with authenticity, integrity, and transparency—aligning their actions with the organization's values and inspiring trust and confidence in others."

The screen displayed images of leaders exemplifying authenticity in their leadership approach. "By staying true to who they are and what they stand for, purpose-driven leaders create a culture of openness, honesty, and accountability, fostering deeper connections and engagement within the organization."

Michael continued, "An authentic leader leads by example, embodying the values and principles they espouse and inspiring others to do the same. Their authenticity builds trust, fosters collaboration, and empowers individuals to unleash their full potential in service of the organization's purpose."

The executives leaned forward, captivated by the transformative power of authenticity in purpose-driven leadership.

"Our journey of purpose-driven leadership also involves **empathy**," Michael said, bringing up an image of a leader listening attentively to their team. "A purpose-driven leader demonstrates empathy and compassion towards others—understanding their needs, motivations, and aspirations, and creating a supportive and inclusive environment where everyone can thrive."

The screen transitioned to a quote by Maya Angelou: "People will forget what you said, people will forget what you did, but people will never forget how you made them feel."

"Angelou's words remind us of the profound impact of empathy in leadership," Michael explained. "By demonstrating empathy and compassion towards others, purpose-driven leaders create a culture of belonging, respect, and support, where individuals feel valued, heard, and empowered to contribute their best."

He paused, allowing the significance of these qualities to sink in. "In conclusion," Michael said, turning off the projector and facing his team, "purpose-driven leadership is not just about achieving success—it's about creating significance. By embracing vision, authenticity, and empathy, we can inspire and empower others to join us on a journey of purpose, impact, and fulfillment."

With a renewed sense of purpose and commitment, the executives at Apex Global Consulting prepared to embrace purpose-driven leadership as their guiding compass, knowing that it held the key to unlocking new levels of alignment, engagement, and impact in their organization.

Case Studies of Purpose-Driven Companies

As the exploration of purpose-driven leadership continued, Michael shifted the focus towards the examination of real-world examples where purpose was deeply embedded in the fabric of organizations. The executives at Apex Global Consulting leaned forward, eager to dissect these case studies and glean insights that would inspire their own purpose-driven journey.

"Let us now turn our attention to case studies of purpose-driven companies," Michael began, his voice infused with excitement and anticipation. "These examples offer us invaluable insights into how purpose can be the driving force behind organizational success, inspiring innovation, engagement, and impact."

He clicked the remote, and the screen displayed the title: **"Case Studies of Purpose-Driven Companies."**

"Our first case study," Michael began, "is that of Patagonia—a global outdoor apparel company that has made environmental sustainability a core part of its business strategy."

The screen transitioned to images of Patagonia's sustainable practices and environmental initiatives. "Patagonia's purpose-driven approach is rooted in its commitment to 'build the best product, cause no unnecessary harm, and use business to inspire and implement solutions to the environmental crisis.'"

Michael continued, "By aligning its business strategies with its purpose of environmental stewardship, Patagonia has not only differentiated itself in the marketplace but has also cultivated a loyal customer base and empowered its employees to drive positive change."

The executives nodded in admiration, recognizing the profound impact of Patagonia's purpose-driven approach.

"Our next case study," Michael said, clicking to the next slide, "is that of TOMS—a footwear company that pioneered the 'One for One' giving model."

The screen displayed images of TOMS' philanthropic initiatives and community impact projects. "TOMS' purpose-driven mission is to 'improve lives through business.' For every pair of shoes purchased, TOMS donates a pair to a person in need, and for every product sold, TOMS helps provide access to clean water, healthcare, and education for people around the world."

Michael continued, "By integrating purpose into its business model, TOMS has not only created a successful and sustainable business but has also transformed the lives of millions of people in need, demonstrating the power of business as a force for good."

The executives sat in awe of TOMS' impactful model, inspired by its commitment to purpose-driven innovation.

"Our final case study," Michael said, clicking to the last slide, "is that of Salesforce—a cloud-based software company that has made social impact a central part of its corporate mission."

The screen displayed images of Salesforce's philanthropic initiatives and employee volunteer programs. "Salesforce's purpose-driven mission is to 'create a more just and equitable world for all.' Through its 1-1-1 model, Salesforce donates 1% of its product, equity, and employee time to support nonprofits and educational institutions."

Michael continued, "By embedding purpose into its corporate culture and operations, Salesforce has not only fostered a sense of purpose and meaning among its employees but has also made a significant impact on the communities it serves, demonstrating the transformative power of purpose-driven leadership."

The executives sat in admiration of Salesforce's commitment to social impact, inspired by its dedication to making a difference in the world.

"In conclusion," Michael said, turning off the projector and facing his team, "these case studies remind us that purpose-driven companies are not only successful in the marketplace but are also agents of positive change in society. By aligning business strategies with purpose, we can create organizations that are not only profitable but also meaningful, impactful, and sustainable."

With a renewed sense of purpose and inspiration, the executives at Apex Global Consulting prepared to integrate the lessons learned from these case studies into their own organizational journey, knowing that purpose-driven leadership held the key to unlocking new levels of success, fulfillment, and impact in their organization.

Measuring and Evaluating Purpose in Business

As the discussion on purpose-driven leadership continued, Michael turned the focus towards the critical task of measuring and evaluating purpose in business—a pivotal step in ensuring that purpose remains at the forefront of organizational strategy and decision-making. The executives at Apex Global Consulting leaned in, eager to uncover the strategies and insights that would help them assess and enhance their organization's purpose-driven efforts.

"Let us now explore the importance of measuring and evaluating purpose in business," Michael began, his voice carrying a sense of urgency and determination. "At the heart of every purpose-driven organization lies a commitment to accountability, transparency, and continuous improvement—a commitment that requires us to measure and evaluate our progress towards fulfilling our mission."

He clicked the remote, and the screen displayed the title: **"Measuring and Evaluating Purpose in Business."**

"Our journey begins with **clarity**," Michael continued, gesturing to the screen. "A clear understanding of what we mean by 'purpose' and how it manifests in our business operations is essential for developing meaningful metrics and evaluation criteria."

The screen transitioned to a quote by Peter Drucker: "What gets measured gets managed."

"Drucker's words remind us of the importance of measurement in driving organizational performance," Michael explained. "By establishing clear metrics and benchmarks for measuring our progress towards fulfilling our purpose, we can ensure that purpose remains a priority in our day-to-day operations and decision-making."

The executives nodded in agreement, recognizing the importance of clarity in measuring purpose in business.

"Next," Michael said, clicking to the next slide, "let us explore the concept of **impact**. Measuring the impact of our purpose-driven initiatives allows us to assess their effectiveness in driving positive change and achieving our mission goals."

The screen displayed images of organizations tracking their social, environmental, and economic impact. "By quantifying the social, environmental, and economic benefits of our purpose-driven efforts, we can demonstrate our organization's value to stakeholders, attract investment, and inspire others to join us in our mission."

Michael continued, "Impact measurement allows us to identify areas of strength and areas for improvement, guiding our strategic decision-making and resource allocation towards maximizing our positive impact."

The executives leaned forward, captivated by the transformative power of impact measurement in driving purpose-driven success.

"Our journey of measuring and evaluating purpose in business also involves **stakeholder engagement**," Michael said, bringing up an image of a diverse group of stakeholders collaborating on a project. "Engaging stakeholders in the measurement and evaluation process ensures that our efforts are aligned with their needs, expectations, and aspirations."

The screen transitioned to a quote by Warren Buffett: "It takes 20 years to build a reputation and five minutes to ruin it. If you think about that, you'll do things differently."

"Buffett's words remind us of the importance of stakeholder trust and confidence in driving organizational success," Michael explained. "By involving stakeholders in the measurement and evaluation of our purpose-driven initiatives, we can build trust, foster collaboration, and ensure that our efforts are responsive to the needs and priorities of those we serve."

He paused, allowing the significance of these strategies to sink in. "In conclusion," Michael said, turning off the projector and facing his team, "measuring and evaluating purpose in business is not just about tracking numbers—it's about driving meaningful change and impact. By embracing clarity, impact measurement, and stakeholder engagement, we can ensure that purpose remains at the heart of our organization's strategy and culture, driving us towards our mission goals and creating a better world for all."

With a renewed sense of purpose and commitment, the executives at Apex Global Consulting prepared to integrate purpose measurement and evaluation into their organization's practices, knowing that it held the key to unlocking new levels of impact, accountability, and success in their purpose-driven journey.

Chapter 5: Decision-Making and Rationality

Philosophical Theories of Decision-Making

In the hushed ambiance of the boardroom, Michael took center stage, ready to unravel the intricate landscape of decision-making and rationality. The executives at Apex Global Consulting leaned forward, eager to grasp the philosophical underpinnings that shape their everyday choices and actions.

"Welcome, everyone, to Chapter 5: Decision-Making and Rationality," Michael began, his voice commanding attention and curiosity. "Today, we embark on a journey into the philosophical theories that illuminate the intricacies of decision-making—the cornerstone of effective leadership and organizational success."

He clicked the remote, and the screen illuminated with the title: **"Philosophical Theories of Decision-Making."**

"Our exploration begins with **rational choice theory**," Michael continued, gesturing towards the screen. "Rational choice theory posits that individuals make decisions by weighing the costs and benefits of available options and selecting the one that maximizes their utility."

The screen transitioned to a quote by Jeremy Bentham: "Nature has placed mankind under the governance of two sovereign masters, pain and pleasure."

"Bentham's words encapsulate the essence of rational choice theory," Michael explained. "According to this perspective, human behavior is driven by the pursuit of pleasure and the avoidance of pain, leading individuals to make decisions that are rational and utility-maximizing."

The executives nodded in recognition, acknowledging the logic behind rational choice theory.

"Next," Michael said, clicking to the next slide, "let us explore the concept of **bounded rationality**. Bounded rationality challenges the notion of perfect rationality, recognizing that human decision-makers are constrained by cognitive limitations, time pressures, and incomplete information."

The screen displayed images of individuals grappling with complex decisions amidst uncertainty and ambiguity. "Bounded rationality acknowledges that decision-makers often rely on heuristics, rules of thumb, and simplifying strategies to navigate the complexities of decision-making, resulting in satisficing rather than optimizing outcomes."

Michael continued, "Herbert Simon, a pioneer of bounded rationality, famously said, 'The cognitive limitations of the human mind make it impossible to attain perfect rationality.'"

The executives leaned forward, captivated by the notion of bounded rationality and its implications for decision-making in the real world.

"Our journey of philosophical theories of decision-making also involves **behavioral economics**," Michael said, bringing up an image of a behavioral economics experiment.

"Behavioral economics integrates insights from psychology and economics to understand how individuals deviate from rational decision-making in systematic and predictable ways."

The screen transitioned to a quote by Daniel Kahneman: "People are generally quite good at coming up with explanations for their behavior after the fact."

"Kahneman's work on prospect theory and cognitive biases sheds light on the irrational tendencies inherent in human decision-making," Michael explained. "From loss aversion to overconfidence to anchoring, behavioral economics reveals the systematic biases that influence our choices and actions, challenging the assumptions of perfect rationality."

He paused, allowing the significance of these theories to sink in. "In conclusion," Michael said, turning off the projector and facing his team, "philosophical theories of decision-making offer us valuable insights into the complexities of human behavior and the challenges of rationality. By embracing concepts such as rational choice theory, bounded rationality, and behavioral economics, we can develop a deeper understanding of decision-making processes and enhance our ability to make effective and informed decisions in the workplace."

With a renewed appreciation for the nuanced nature of decision-making, the executives at Apex Global Consulting prepared to apply these philosophical insights to their leadership roles, knowing that they held the key to navigating the complexities of the business world with wisdom and clarity.

Rational Decision-Making Models

Continuing their exploration into the intricate world of decision-making, Michael shifted the focus towards the examination of rational decision-making models—a cornerstone of organizational strategy and leadership. The executives at Apex Global Consulting leaned in, eager to dissect these models and glean insights that would sharpen their decision-making prowess.

"Let us now delve into the realm of rational decision-making models," Michael began, his voice carrying a tone of analytical precision and curiosity. "These models provide structured frameworks for evaluating alternatives, weighing risks and rewards, and making optimal choices—a vital skill for effective leadership in today's complex business environment."

He clicked the remote, and the screen illuminated with the title: **"Rational Decision-Making Models."**

"Our journey begins with the **classical economic model**," Michael continued, gesturing towards the screen. "Rooted in rational choice theory, the classical economic model assumes that decision-makers have complete information, unlimited cognitive abilities, and consistent preferences, enabling them to make optimal choices that maximize utility."

The screen transitioned to a diagram illustrating the steps of the classical economic model: identifying alternatives, evaluating criteria, weighting trade-offs, and selecting the best option. "According to this model, decision-makers carefully assess the costs and benefits of available options, consider all relevant information, and choose the alternative that offers the highest expected utility."

The executives nodded in recognition, familiar with the

logical underpinnings of the classical economic model.

"Next," Michael said, clicking to the next slide, "let us explore the concept of **expected utility theory**. Expected utility theory extends the principles of rational choice theory by incorporating probabilistic outcomes and risk preferences into decision-making."

The screen displayed images of decision trees and utility curves, illustrating the mathematical calculations involved in expected utility theory. "According to expected utility theory, decision-makers assign probabilities to possible outcomes, assess the utility or value associated with each outcome, and select the alternative that maximizes their expected utility."

Michael continued, "By quantifying the risks and rewards of available options, expected utility theory provides decision-makers with a systematic approach to making decisions under uncertainty, allowing them to balance risks and rewards and make informed choices."

The executives leaned forward, intrigued by the mathematical rigor of expected utility theory and its practical implications for decision-making.

"Our journey of rational decision-making models also involves **decision analysis**," Michael said, bringing up an image of a decision matrix. "Decision analysis is a systematic approach to evaluating alternatives, identifying objectives, and assessing trade-offs in decision-making."

The screen transitioned to a quote by Howard Raiffa: "The most important step in decision-making is to define the problem."

"Raiffa's words highlight the importance of clarity and precision in decision analysis," Michael explained. "By breaking down complex decisions into smaller, manageable components, decision analysis helps decision-makers identify their objectives, evaluate the consequences of their choices, and select the alternative that best aligns with their goals."

He paused, allowing the significance of these models to sink in. "In conclusion," Michael said, turning off the projector and facing his team, "rational decision-making models provide us with valuable tools for navigating the complexities of decision-making in the workplace. By embracing concepts such as the classical economic model, expected utility theory, and decision analysis, we can enhance our ability to make informed, effective, and rational decisions that drive organizational success."

With a renewed appreciation for the structured frameworks of rational decision-making, the executives at Apex Global Consulting prepared to apply these models to their decision-making processes, knowing that they held the key to navigating the complexities of the business world with clarity and precision.

The Role of Intuition and Emotion in Decisions

Continuing their journey through the intricacies of decision-making, Michael turned the spotlight towards the often overlooked role of intuition and emotion—a dynamic interplay that shapes our choices in profound ways. The executives at Apex Global Consulting leaned forward, eager to unravel the mysteries of intuition and emotion and their impact on their decision-making processes.

"Let us now explore the nuanced interplay of intuition and emotion in decisions," Michael began, his voice carrying a tone of curiosity and introspection. "These aspects of human psychology offer valuable insights into the complexities of decision-making, challenging the assumptions of rationality and logic that often dominate our understanding."

He clicked the remote, and the screen illuminated with the title: **"The Role of Intuition and Emotion in Decisions."**

"Our journey begins with **intuition**," Michael continued, gesturing towards the screen. "Intuition is the ability to understand or know something instinctively, without the need for conscious reasoning. It operates at a subconscious level, drawing upon our past experiences, knowledge, and expertise to guide our decisions in the present moment."

The screen transitioned to a quote by Albert Einstein: "The intuitive mind is a sacred gift and the rational mind is a faithful servant. We have created a society that honors the servant and has forgotten the gift."

"Einstein's words remind us of the inherent value of intuition in decision-making," Michael explained. "Intuition allows us to quickly assess complex situations, recognize patterns, and make rapid decisions based on our gut feelings and instincts."

The executives nodded in recognition, acknowledging the intuitive leaps that often underlie their most impactful decisions.

"Next," Michael said, clicking to the next slide, "let us explore the concept of **emotions**. Emotions play a significant role in decision-making, influencing our perceptions, judgments, and choices in profound ways."

The screen displayed images of individuals experiencing a range of emotions, from joy and excitement to fear and anxiety. "Emotions serve as powerful signals that alert us to potential risks and opportunities, guiding our decisions towards outcomes that align with our emotional states."

Michael continued, "From the thrill of a successful business deal to the fear of failure, emotions shape our attitudes and behaviors, influencing the decisions we make and the actions we take in the workplace."

The executives leaned forward, captivated by the intricate dance of emotions and their impact on their decision-making processes.

"Our journey of understanding the role of intuition and emotion in decisions also involves **emotional intelligence**," Michael said, bringing up an image of a team engaging in emotional intelligence training. "Emotional intelligence is the ability to recognize, understand, and manage our own emotions, as well as the emotions of others."

The screen transitioned to a quote by Daniel Goleman: "In a very real sense we have two minds, one that thinks and one that feels."

"Goleman's words highlight the importance of emotional intelligence in decision-making," Michael explained. "By cultivating emotional intelligence, we can develop greater self-awareness, empathy, and social skills, enabling us to make more informed, adaptive, and empathetic decisions in the workplace."

He paused, allowing the significance of intuition and emotion to sink in. "In conclusion," Michael said, turning off the projector and facing his team, "intuition and emotion are integral aspects of decision-making, offering valuable insights and guiding our choices in profound ways. By embracing these aspects of human psychology and cultivating emotional intelligence, we can enhance our ability to make informed, adaptive, and empathetic decisions that drive organizational success."

With a renewed appreciation for the complexities of decision-making, the executives at Apex Global Consulting prepared to integrate the lessons learned about intuition and emotion into their decision-making processes, knowing that they held the key to navigating the complexities of the business world with wisdom and empathy.

Ethical Implications of Decision-Making

As the discussion on decision-making unfolded, Michael shifted the focus towards the ethical dimensions that permeate every choice and action. The executives at Apex Global Consulting leaned in, recognizing the profound implications of ethical considerations in their decision-making processes.

"Let us now delve into the ethical implications of decision-making," Michael began, his voice resonating with gravitas and introspection. "Ethics serve as the moral compass that guides our decisions, ensuring that we uphold principles of integrity, fairness, and responsibility in our actions."

He clicked the remote, and the screen illuminated with the title: **"Ethical Implications of Decision-Making."**

"Our journey begins with **integrity**," Michael continued, gesturing towards the screen. "Integrity is the cornerstone of ethical decision-making, requiring us to act with honesty, transparency, and consistency in all our dealings."

The screen transitioned to a quote by Warren Buffett: "In looking for people to hire, you look for three qualities: integrity, intelligence, and energy. And if they don't have the first, the other two will kill you."

"Buffett's words remind us of the paramount importance of integrity in decision-making," Michael explained. "By acting with integrity, we uphold the trust and confidence of our stakeholders, foster a culture of accountability and respect, and maintain the reputation and credibility of our organization."

The executives nodded in agreement, recognizing the foundational role of integrity in ethical decision-making.

"Next," Michael said, clicking to the next slide, "let us explore the concept of **fairness**. Fairness requires us to consider the interests and rights of all stakeholders affected by our decisions, ensuring that our actions are just, equitable, and inclusive."

The screen displayed images of individuals engaging in dialogue and negotiation, seeking to balance competing interests and perspectives. "Fairness compels us to engage in open and transparent decision-making processes, listen to diverse viewpoints, and strive for outcomes that promote the common good and uphold principles of social justice."

Michael continued, "By prioritizing fairness in our decision-making, we can build trust, strengthen relationships, and foster a culture of collaboration and mutual respect within our organization and beyond."

The executives leaned forward, captivated by the notion of fairness and its implications for their decision-making processes.

"Our journey of ethical decision-making also involves **responsibility**," Michael said, bringing up an image of a person holding the world in their hands. "Responsibility requires us to consider the broader impact of our decisions on society, the environment, and future generations, ensuring that we act in ways that are sustainable, ethical, and socially responsible."

The screen transitioned to a quote by Mahatma Gandhi: "The best way to find yourself is to lose yourself in the service of others."

"Gandhi's words remind us of the ethical imperative to act in service of others," Michael explained. "By embracing responsibility in our decision-making, we can create value for society, protect the planet, and contribute to the well-being and prosperity of present and future generations."

He paused, allowing the significance of ethical considerations to sink in. "In conclusion," Michael said, turning off the projector and facing his team, "ethical decision-making is not just about following rules or avoiding harm—it's about embodying principles of integrity, fairness, and responsibility in all our actions. By embracing these ethical values, we can make decisions that not only drive organizational success but also contribute to a more just, sustainable, and compassionate world."

With a renewed commitment to ethical decision-making, the executives at Apex Global Consulting prepared to integrate these principles into their decision-making processes, knowing that they held the key to creating a positive impact in their organization and beyond.

Case Studies on Decision-Making in Management

As the discussion on decision-making continued, Michael shifted the focus towards the exploration of real-world case studies—a captivating journey into the complexities and nuances of decision-making in management. The executives at Apex Global Consulting leaned in, eager to dissect these cases and glean insights that would sharpen their decision-making acumen.

"Let us now turn our attention to case studies on decision-making in management," Michael began, his voice infused with anticipation and curiosity. "These examples offer us invaluable lessons and perspectives on the challenges, dilemmas, and strategies involved in making critical decisions that shape the course of organizations."

He clicked the remote, and the screen illuminated with the title: **"Case Studies on Decision-Making in Management."**

"Our journey begins with the case of **Johnson & Johnson's Tylenol Crisis**," Michael continued, gesturing towards the screen. "In 1982, seven people died after consuming Tylenol capsules that had been laced with cyanide—a crisis that threatened the reputation and viability of the brand."

The screen transitioned to images of Tylenol products and news headlines about the crisis. "In response to the crisis, Johnson & Johnson faced a critical decision: whether to recall all Tylenol products or continue with business as usual."

Michael continued, "By prioritizing public safety and transparency over short-term financial considerations, Johnson & Johnson made the bold decision to recall 31 million bottles of Tylenol, costing the company millions of dollars but ultimately preserving its reputation and earning the trust and loyalty of consumers."

The executives nodded in admiration, recognizing the courage and integrity demonstrated by Johnson & Johnson in the face of adversity.

"Our next case study," Michael said, clicking to the next slide, "is that of **Netflix's Expansion into Original Content**."

The screen displayed images of Netflix's original series and movies, along with charts showing the growth of its subscriber base. "In 2013, Netflix faced a critical decision: whether to expand into original content production—a risky endeavor that required significant investment and posed challenges to its existing business model."

Michael continued, "By recognizing the shifting landscape of the entertainment industry and the importance of differentiation in a crowded market, Netflix made the strategic decision to produce original content, leading to the creation of hit series like 'House of Cards' and 'Stranger Things' and solidifying its position as a leader in the streaming industry."

The executives leaned forward, captivated by Netflix's bold strategy and its transformative impact on the entertainment landscape.

"Our final case study," Michael said, clicking to the last slide, "is that of **Apple's Decision to Remove the Headphone Jack from the iPhone**."

The screen displayed images of iPhones and headlines about the controversial decision. "In 2016, Apple faced backlash and skepticism after announcing its decision to remove the headphone jack from the iPhone 7—a move that sparked debate among consumers and industry experts."

Michael continued, "By prioritizing innovation and user experience over tradition and convenience, Apple made the strategic decision to embrace wireless technology, paving the way for future advancements in mobile connectivity and positioning itself as a trendsetter in the tech industry."

The executives sat in awe of Apple's visionary decision-making and its transformative impact on the smartphone market.

"In conclusion," Michael said, turning off the projector and facing his team, "these case studies remind us that decision-making in management is not just about choosing between options—it's about navigating uncertainty, balancing risks and rewards, and staying true to our values and vision. By learning from the experiences of others, we can gain valuable insights and perspectives that inform our own decision-making processes, driving organizational success and innovation."

With a renewed appreciation for the complexities of decision-making, the executives at Apex Global Consulting prepared to integrate the lessons learned from these case studies into their own decision-making practices, knowing that they held the key to navigating the challenges and opportunities of the business world with wisdom and foresight.

Tools for Improving Decision-Making

As the discussion on decision-making continued, Michael shifted the focus towards the exploration of practical tools and techniques—an empowering journey into the arsenal of resources available to enhance decision-making processes. The executives at Apex Global Consulting leaned in, eager to discover the tools that would sharpen their decision-making acumen and drive organizational success.

"Let us now delve into the array of tools available for improving decision-making," Michael began, his voice infused with a sense of anticipation and determination. "These tools offer us practical strategies and frameworks to navigate the complexities of decision-making, empowering us to make more informed, effective, and strategic choices."

He clicked the remote, and the screen illuminated with the title: **"Tools for Improving Decision-Making."**

"Our journey begins with the **decision matrix**," Michael continued, gesturing towards the screen. "The decision matrix is a systematic tool for evaluating alternatives based on multiple criteria, helping decision-makers identify the most viable option that aligns with their objectives."

The screen transitioned to a visual representation of a decision matrix, with rows and columns listing alternatives and criteria. "By assigning weights to criteria and scoring alternatives based on their performance, decision-makers can quantitatively assess the relative merits of each option and make data-driven decisions that maximize value and minimize risk."

The executives nodded in recognition, recognizing the value of the decision matrix in structuring their decision-making processes.

"Next," Michael said, clicking to the next slide, "let us explore the concept of **scenario planning**. Scenario planning is a strategic tool for anticipating future uncertainties and developing contingency plans to mitigate risks and capitalize on opportunities."

The screen displayed images of individuals engaged in scenario planning exercises, mapping out different future scenarios and their potential implications. "By envisioning alternative futures, identifying key drivers of change, and assessing their potential impacts, organizations can prepare for a range of possible outcomes and adapt their strategies accordingly."

Michael continued, "Scenario planning enables decision-makers to navigate uncertainty with confidence, fostering resilience and agility in the face of complex and dynamic environments."

CHAPTER 5: DECISION-MAKING AND RATIONALITY

The executives leaned forward, captivated by the strategic foresight offered by scenario planning.

"Our journey of tools for improving decision-making also involves **decision trees**," Michael said, bringing up an image of a decision tree diagram. "Decision trees are graphical representations of decision-making processes, depicting the sequence of choices and their potential outcomes in a hierarchical structure."

The screen transitioned to a visual representation of a decision tree, with branches representing different decision options and nodes representing possible outcomes. "By mapping out decision pathways and calculating expected values at each decision point, decision trees help decision-makers identify the most favorable course of action and quantify the risks and rewards associated with each option."

He paused, allowing the significance of these tools to sink in. "In conclusion," Michael said, turning off the projector and facing his team, "tools for improving decision-making offer us invaluable resources for navigating the complexities of the business world with clarity and confidence. By embracing tools such as the decision matrix, scenario planning, and decision trees, we can enhance our ability to make informed, strategic, and impactful decisions that drive organizational success and innovation."

With a renewed appreciation for the practical tools at their disposal, the executives at Apex Global Consulting prepared to integrate these techniques into their decision-making processes, knowing that they held the key to unlocking new levels of effectiveness and strategic insight in their organization.

Chapter 6: Justice and Fairness in the Workplace

Philosophical Concepts of Justice and Fairness

As the discussion progressed into Chapter 6, the atmosphere in the boardroom at Apex Global Consulting became one of introspection and gravity. Michael stood before the group, ready to delve into the profound and nuanced concepts of justice and fairness in the workplace. The executives, sensing the importance of this topic, leaned in with anticipation.

"Today, we embark on a crucial journey into the heart of organizational ethics," Michael began, his voice resonating with solemnity. "Justice and fairness are not just abstract principles—they are the foundation upon which trust, respect, and collaboration are built within any organization."

He clicked the remote, and the screen illuminated with the title: **"Justice and Fairness in the Workplace."**

"Our journey begins with understanding the **philosophical concepts of justice and fairness**," Michael continued, gesturing towards the screen. "These concepts have been debated and refined by philosophers for centuries, and their insights offer invaluable guidance for creating equitable and just workplaces."

The screen transitioned to a quote by John Rawls: "Justice is the first virtue of social institutions, as truth is of systems of thought."

"Rawls's words remind us of the paramount importance of justice in shaping our social and organizational structures," Michael explained. "His theory of justice as fairness emphasizes the need to design systems and policies that ensure equal opportunities and fair treatment for all individuals, regardless of their background or circumstances."

The screen displayed an image of Rawls's famous "veil of ignorance" thought experiment. "According to Rawls, we should design our institutions as if we were behind a veil of ignorance, unaware of our own place in society. This ensures that our decisions are fair and impartial, promoting equality and justice for all."

The executives nodded thoughtfully, reflecting on the implications of Rawls's theory for their own organization.

"Next," Michael said, clicking to the next slide, "let us explore the concept of **distributive justice**. Distributive justice concerns the fair allocation of resources, opportunities, and rewards within an organization."

The screen displayed images of various individuals receiving equal pay for equal work and opportunities for advancement. "Philosophers like Aristotle have argued that distributive justice requires us to distribute benefits and burdens in proportion to individuals' contributions and needs. This means ensuring that our reward systems are fair and equitable, recognizing both merit and necessity."

Michael continued, "By embracing distributive justice, we

can create a workplace where individuals feel valued and respected, fostering a culture of trust and collaboration."

The executives leaned forward, considering how to implement distributive justice in their reward and recognition systems.

"Our journey also involves the concept of **procedural justice**," Michael said, bringing up an image of a fair and transparent decision-making process. "Procedural justice focuses on the fairness of the processes and procedures used to make decisions, rather than the outcomes themselves."

The screen transitioned to a quote by Tom R. Tyler: "When people perceive the procedures used to make decisions as fair, they are more likely to accept and comply with the outcomes, even if they are unfavorable."

"Tyler's research highlights the importance of transparency, consistency, and impartiality in decision-making processes," Michael explained. "By ensuring that our procedures are fair, we can build trust and legitimacy, encouraging employees to accept and support organizational decisions."

He paused, allowing the significance of these philosophical concepts to sink in. "In conclusion," Michael said, turning off the projector and facing his team, "the philosophical concepts of justice and fairness offer us profound insights into creating equitable and just workplaces. By embracing principles of distributive and procedural justice, we can foster a culture of trust, respect, and collaboration, ensuring that all individuals are treated with dignity and fairness."

With a renewed commitment to justice and fairness, the executives at Apex Global Consulting prepared to integrate these philosophical principles into their organizational practices, knowing that they held the key to building a more just and equitable workplace.

Applying Justice in Management Practices

As the discussion deepened into the realm of justice and fairness, Michael pivoted towards the practical application of these philosophical principles in management practices. The executives at Apex Global Consulting, understanding the gravity of this endeavor, prepared to explore how to translate lofty ideals into tangible actions.

"Now that we have explored the philosophical underpinnings of justice and fairness," Michael began, his voice filled with determination, "let us turn our focus to the application of these principles in our day-to-day management practices."

He clicked the remote, and the screen illuminated with the title: **"Applying Justice in Management Practices."**

"Our journey begins with **recruitment and hiring practices**," Michael continued, gesturing towards the screen. "To ensure justice and fairness, we must design processes that provide equal opportunities for all candidates, regardless of their background or circumstances."

The screen transitioned to images of diverse candidates in a fair interview setting. "Implementing structured interviews, using standardized criteria for evaluation, and promoting blind recruitment practices are crucial steps. These measures help eliminate biases and ensure that all candidates are assessed based on their qualifications and potential."

The executives nodded thoughtfully, recognizing the importance of fair recruitment in building a diverse and inclusive workforce.

"Next," Michael said, clicking to the next slide, "let us

explore **performance evaluations**. Fair and transparent performance evaluations are essential for maintaining trust and morale within the organization."

The screen displayed images of performance review meetings and balanced scorecards. "To apply justice in performance evaluations, we must use objective criteria, provide regular feedback, and ensure that employees have the opportunity to participate in the process. This means setting clear goals, using measurable performance indicators, and offering constructive feedback that supports employee development."

Michael continued, "By ensuring that our performance evaluations are fair and transparent, we can recognize and reward employees based on their true contributions, fostering a culture of meritocracy and trust."

The executives leaned forward, considering how to enhance their performance evaluation processes to reflect these principles.

"Our journey also involves **promotions and career advancement**," Michael said, bringing up an image of a diverse group of employees climbing a career ladder. "Promotions should be based on merit, potential, and equitable opportunities for growth."

The screen transitioned to a quote by Peter Drucker: "The task of leadership is to create an alignment of strengths, making a system's weaknesses irrelevant."

"Drucker's words remind us that promoting justice in career advancement requires us to focus on individuals' strengths and potential," Michael explained. "We must ensure that all employees have access to professional development opportunities, mentorship, and clear pathways for advancement."

He paused, letting the significance of fair career advancement resonate with the team. "In conclusion," Michael said, turning off the projector and facing his team, "applying justice in management practices involves embedding principles of fairness and equity into every aspect of our organizational processes. By ensuring that our recruitment, performance evaluations, and promotions are just and fair, we can create a workplace where all individuals have the opportunity to thrive and succeed."

With a renewed commitment to applying justice in their management practices, the executives at Apex Global Consulting prepared to integrate these principles into their organizational strategies, knowing that they held the key to building a more equitable and inclusive workplace.

Disruptive Justice Organizations

As the exploration of justice and fairness in management practices progressed, Michael turned his attention to the concept of disruptive justice organizations—entities that challenge traditional norms and strive for radical equity and inclusion. The executives at Apex Global Consulting were intrigued, ready to learn from the bold examples of these pioneering organizations.

"Having discussed the philosophical concepts and practical applications of justice, let's now delve into the realm of **disruptive justice organizations**," Michael began, his voice charged with excitement. "These organizations are not content with incremental change; they seek to fundamentally reshape their industries and societies by embedding radical principles of justice and fairness into their core operations."

He clicked the remote, and the screen illuminated with the

title: **"Disruptive Justice Organizations."**

"Our journey begins with the case of **Patagonia**," Michael continued, gesturing towards the screen. "Patagonia is a company renowned for its commitment to environmental and social justice. They have disrupted the traditional business model by integrating sustainability and ethical practices into every aspect of their operations."

The screen transitioned to images of Patagonia's sustainable products and activism campaigns. "Patagonia donates a significant portion of its profits to environmental causes, advocates for fair labor practices, and encourages customers to buy less by promoting the repair and reuse of their products."

Michael continued, "By challenging the conventional consumerism-driven business model, Patagonia not only prioritizes environmental justice but also inspires other companies to adopt more sustainable and ethical practices."

The executives nodded in admiration, recognizing the boldness and impact of Patagonia's approach.

"Next," Michael said, clicking to the next slide, "let us explore **Ben & Jerry's**. This ice cream company has made social justice a central pillar of its brand and operations."

The screen displayed images of Ben & Jerry's social justice campaigns and community initiatives. "Ben & Jerry's uses its platform to advocate for various social causes, from racial justice to climate change. They actively engage in political advocacy, partner with grassroots organizations, and educate their customers about social issues."

Michael continued, "By leveraging their brand for social good, Ben & Jerry's demonstrates that businesses can be powerful agents of change, promoting justice and equity on a larger scale."

CHAPTER 6: JUSTICE AND FAIRNESS IN THE WORKPLACE

The executives leaned forward, captivated by Ben & Jerry's commitment to social activism.

"Our journey also involves **Warby Parker**," Michael said, bringing up an image of Warby Parker's eyewear and their 'Buy a Pair, Give a Pair' program. "Warby Parker disrupted the eyewear industry with their innovative business model and commitment to social impact."

The screen transitioned to visuals of Warby Parker's initiatives in underserved communities. "For every pair of glasses sold, Warby Parker donates a pair to someone in need. They also invest in programs that train individuals to conduct eye exams and provide affordable eyewear in developing countries."

Michael explained, "By integrating social justice into their business model, Warby Parker not only addresses a critical health need but also challenges the status quo in the eyewear industry."

He paused, allowing the significance of these disruptive justice organizations to resonate with the team. "In conclusion," Michael said, turning off the projector and facing his team, "disruptive justice organizations like Patagonia, Ben & Jerry's, and Warby Parker show us that it is possible to achieve both business success and social impact. By challenging traditional norms and prioritizing justice and fairness, these organizations pave the way for a more equitable and sustainable future."

With a renewed sense of inspiration and determination, the executives at Apex Global Consulting prepared to integrate the lessons learned from these disruptive justice organizations into their own strategies, knowing that they held the key to driving transformative change in their industry and beyond.

Procedural Justice in Decision-Making

As the exploration of justice and fairness in management practices continued, Michael shifted the focus to the critical aspect of procedural justice in decision-making. The executives at Apex Global Consulting sensed the importance of this topic, understanding that fair processes are fundamental to fostering trust and legitimacy within the organization.

"Having examined disruptive justice organizations, let's now turn our attention to the importance of **procedural justice in decision-making**," Michael began, his voice steady and clear. "Procedural justice focuses on the fairness of the processes and procedures used to make decisions, rather than just the outcomes themselves."

He clicked the remote, and the screen illuminated with the title: "**Procedural Justice in Decision-Making.**"

"Our journey begins with understanding the core principles of procedural justice," Michael continued, gesturing towards the screen. "These principles include consistency, transparency, voice, and impartiality. By adhering to these principles, we can ensure that our decision-making processes are perceived as fair and legitimate by all stakeholders."

The screen transitioned to a visual representation of these principles: a balanced scale with each principle highlighted. "Consistency means applying rules and procedures uniformly across all cases. Transparency involves openly sharing the criteria and processes used to make decisions. Voice ensures that all affected parties have the opportunity to express their views and concerns. Impartiality requires decision-makers to be neutral and unbiased."

The executives nodded thoughtfully, recognizing the foundational role of these principles in fostering a fair organizational culture.

"Next," Michael said, clicking to the next slide, "let us explore how these principles can be applied in practical scenarios. Consider the example of **employee promotions**."

The screen displayed images of employees engaged in a transparent and participatory promotion process. "When making promotion decisions, it's crucial to establish clear, objective criteria that are communicated to all employees. Regular feedback and performance reviews should be conducted to ensure that employees understand how they are evaluated and what they need to do to advance."

Michael continued, "By involving employees in the promotion process, soliciting their feedback, and providing them with a platform to express their views, we ensure that the process is transparent and inclusive. This fosters trust and morale, as employees feel that they are treated fairly and have a say in their career progression."

The executives leaned forward, considering how to enhance their promotion processes to reflect these principles.

"Our journey also involves **disciplinary actions**," Michael said, bringing up an image of a fair and transparent disciplinary process. "Procedural justice is critical when dealing with disciplinary issues. This means having clear policies in place, conducting thorough and unbiased investigations, and ensuring that the affected parties have an opportunity to present their side of the story."

The screen transitioned to a quote by Tom R. Tyler: "When people perceive the procedures used to make decisions as fair, they are more likely to accept and comply with the outcomes, even if they are unfavorable."

"Tyler's research highlights the importance of procedural fairness in gaining acceptance and compliance with decisions," Michael explained. "By ensuring that our disciplinary processes are consistent, transparent, and impartial, we can maintain trust and legitimacy within the organization."

He paused, allowing the significance of procedural justice to resonate with the team. "In conclusion," Michael said, turning off the projector and facing his team, "procedural justice in decision-making is not just about following rules—it's about creating processes that are fair, transparent, and inclusive. By embracing the principles of consistency, transparency, voice, and impartiality, we can build a culture of trust and respect, ensuring that all individuals feel valued and fairly treated."

With a renewed commitment to procedural justice, the executives at Apex Global Consulting prepared to integrate these principles into their decision-making processes, knowing that they held the key to fostering a more just and equitable workplace.

Case Studies of Fairness in the Workplace

As the exploration of justice and fairness in the workplace continued, Michael decided to bring the principles to life through real-world examples. The executives at Apex Global Consulting were eager to learn from the successes and challenges of other organizations that had prioritized fairness in their practices.

"Now that we have discussed the philosophical foundations and practical applications of justice, let's examine some **case studies of fairness in the workplace**," Michael began, his voice filled with anticipation. "These case studies will provide us with concrete examples of how organizations have implemented fairness and the impact it has had on their culture and success."

He clicked the remote, and the screen illuminated with the title: **"Case Studies of Fairness in the Workplace."**

"Our first case study is **Starbucks**," Michael continued, gesturing towards the screen. "Starbucks has been recognized for its efforts to create a fair and inclusive workplace, particularly through its employee benefits and training programs."

The screen transitioned to images of Starbucks employees and their comprehensive benefits package. "Starbucks offers its employees, whom it refers to as 'partners,' extensive benefits including healthcare, tuition assistance, and stock options. Additionally, the company has implemented robust training programs to promote diversity and inclusion, as well as unconscious bias training."

Michael continued, "By investing in its employees' well-being and professional development, Starbucks fosters a culture of fairness and inclusivity, which in turn enhances employee loyalty and customer satisfaction."

The executives nodded, recognizing the positive impact of Starbucks' commitment to fairness on its overall success.

"Next," Michael said, clicking to the next slide, "let us explore the case of **Salesforce**. This tech giant has made significant strides in promoting pay equity and transparency within its organization."

The screen displayed images of Salesforce's headquarters and their pay equity initiatives. "Salesforce conducts regular pay audits to ensure that employees are compensated fairly regardless of gender, race, or ethnicity. When discrepancies are found, the company makes immediate adjustments to rectify them."

Michael continued, "By prioritizing pay equity and transparency, Salesforce not only addresses systemic inequalities but also builds trust and morale among its workforce. This commitment to fairness has positioned Salesforce as a leader in the tech industry and an employer of choice."

The executives leaned forward, captivated by Salesforce's proactive approach to ensuring fair compensation.

"Our journey also involves the case of **The Body Shop**," Michael said, bringing up an image of The Body Shop's ethical and fair trade practices. "The Body Shop has long been a pioneer in promoting ethical sourcing and fair trade, ensuring that its suppliers and workers are treated fairly and ethically."

The screen transitioned to visuals of fair trade products and community development initiatives supported by The Body Shop. "The company partners with communities around the world to source ingredients ethically, providing fair wages and supporting local development projects. This not only ensures fair treatment of suppliers but also strengthens the sustainability of their supply chain."

Michael explained, "By integrating fairness into their sourcing practices, The Body Shop builds strong, ethical relationships with suppliers and contributes to positive social impact globally."

He paused, allowing the significance of these case studies to resonate with the team. "In conclusion," Michael said, turning off the projector and facing his team, "these case studies of fairness in the workplace demonstrate the transformative power of prioritizing justice and equity. Organizations like Starbucks, Salesforce, and The Body Shop show us that fairness is not just a moral imperative but also a strategic advantage that drives employee engagement, customer loyalty, and overall success."

With a renewed sense of inspiration and commitment to fairness, the executives at Apex Global Consulting prepared to integrate the lessons learned from these case studies into their own practices, knowing that they held the key to building a more just and equitable workplace.

Strategies for Promoting Justice in Organizations

As the discussion on justice and fairness reached its climax, Michael prepared to equip the executives at Apex Global Consulting with actionable strategies to promote justice within their organization. The room was filled with a palpable sense of anticipation as everyone leaned in, ready to transform principles into practice.

"We have explored the theoretical foundations, practical applications, and inspiring case studies of justice in the workplace," Michael began, his voice resonant with purpose. "Now, it's time to turn our attention to **strategies for promoting justice in organizations**. These strategies will guide us in embedding fairness into the fabric of our organizational culture."

He clicked the remote, and the screen illuminated with the title: **"Strategies for Promoting Justice in Organizations."**

"Our first strategy is to **establish clear and transparent policies**," Michael continued, gesturing towards the screen. "Clear policies are the bedrock of fairness. They set expectations, provide guidelines for behavior, and ensure consistency in decision-making."

The screen transitioned to an image of a well-documented

policy manual. "To achieve this, we must develop comprehensive policies that cover all aspects of organizational operations, from recruitment and promotions to conflict resolution and performance evaluations. These policies should be accessible to all employees and communicated regularly to ensure everyone understands them."

The executives nodded, recognizing the importance of clear and transparent policies in fostering a fair workplace.

"Next," Michael said, clicking to the next slide, "we need to **implement training programs on justice and fairness**. Training is essential to educate employees about the principles of justice and how to apply them in their daily interactions."

The screen displayed images of employees participating in interactive training sessions. "These programs should cover topics such as unconscious bias, ethical decision-making, and inclusive leadership. By providing regular training, we equip our employees with the knowledge and skills to uphold justice in all their actions."

Michael continued, "Training also fosters a shared understanding and commitment to fairness, creating a cohesive and inclusive organizational culture."

The executives leaned forward, considering how to design and implement effective training programs within their own teams.

"Our journey also involves **creating mechanisms for employee voice and participation**," Michael said, bringing up an image of a town hall meeting. "Giving employees a platform to express their views and participate in decision-making processes is crucial for promoting procedural justice."

The screen transitioned to visuals of suggestion boxes, feedback forms, and employee councils. "We can establish regular town hall meetings, anonymous feedback channels, and employee resource groups. These mechanisms ensure that employees feel heard and valued, and their input is considered in shaping organizational policies and decisions."

Michael explained, "By fostering an environment where employees can freely share their perspectives, we enhance transparency, trust, and engagement."

He paused, letting the significance of these strategies resonate with the team. "Another key strategy is to **ensure accountability and fair enforcement of policies**," Michael said, clicking to the next slide. "Accountability mechanisms are vital for maintaining fairness and justice."

The screen displayed images of an independent ethics committee and a whistleblower protection program. "We can establish independent committees to oversee policy enforcement, conduct regular audits, and investigate complaints impartially. Additionally, protecting whistleblowers who report unethical behavior is essential for encouraging transparency and accountability."

Michael continued, "By ensuring that policies are enforced fairly and consistently, we build trust and credibility within the organization."

The executives nodded thoughtfully, acknowledging the importance of accountability in promoting justice.

"In conclusion," Michael said, turning off the projector and facing his team, "promoting justice in organizations requires a multifaceted approach. By establishing clear policies, implementing training programs, creating mechanisms for employee voice, and ensuring accountability, we can build a culture of fairness and equity."

With a renewed sense of purpose and determination, the

executives at Apex Global Consulting prepared to integrate these strategies into their organizational practices, knowing that they held the key to fostering a more just and equitable workplace.

Chapter 7: Corporate Social Responsibility (CSR)

Philosophical Underpinnings of CSR

As the discussion at Apex Global Consulting transitioned to the next major topic, the room buzzed with anticipation. Michael stood at the front, ready to dive into the complexities and importance of Corporate Social Responsibility (CSR). The executives were eager to understand how philosophical principles underpin CSR and guide ethical business practices.

"Today, we explore a vital aspect of modern business— **Corporate Social Responsibility (CSR)**," Michael began, his voice commanding attention. "CSR is more than just a business strategy; it's a moral obligation rooted in deep philosophical principles."

He clicked the remote, and the screen illuminated with the title: "**Corporate Social Responsibility (CSR).**"

"Our journey begins with the **philosophical underpinnings of CSR**," Michael continued, gesturing towards the screen. "Understanding these principles is crucial for grasping why CSR is not just beneficial, but essential for any forward-thinking organization."

The screen transitioned to a quote by Immanuel Kant: "Act only according to that maxim whereby you can at the same time will that it should become a universal law."

"Kant's categorical imperative provides a foundation for ethical behavior in business," Michael explained. "It challenges us to act in ways that we would want to become universal norms. In the context of CSR, this means considering the broader impact of our actions on society and the environment, and striving to make positive contributions that could serve as a model for others."

The executives nodded, absorbing the profound ethical implications of their corporate actions.

"Next," Michael said, clicking to the next slide, "we delve into the concept of **utilitarianism**, as proposed by John Stuart Mill. Utilitarianism advocates for actions that maximize overall happiness and minimize suffering."

The screen displayed an image of a balanced scale with happiness and suffering on either side. "In terms of CSR, this means evaluating our business decisions based on their impact on all stakeholders—employees, customers, communities, and the environment. Our goal should be to maximize the positive outcomes of our actions and minimize any negative consequences."

Michael continued, "By adopting a utilitarian approach, we ensure that our business practices contribute to the greater good, fostering trust and goodwill among our stakeholders."

The executives leaned forward, considering how to implement these ethical considerations in their strategic planning.

"Our journey also involves the **theory of justice** as articulated by John Rawls," Michael said, bringing up an image of Rawls's famous 'veil of ignorance' thought experiment. "Rawls's principles of justice as fairness challenge us to design systems and policies that we would consider fair if we were ignorant of our own position in society."

The screen transitioned to visuals of equitable resource distribution and community support initiatives. "Applying this theory to CSR means ensuring that our corporate policies and practices promote fairness and equity. This includes providing fair wages, ensuring safe working conditions, and engaging in practices that benefit marginalized and underserved communities."

Michael explained, "By embedding Rawls's principles into our CSR initiatives, we commit to creating a more just and equitable society."

He paused, allowing the significance of these philosophical theories to resonate with the team. "In conclusion," Michael said, turning off the projector and facing his team, "the philosophical underpinnings of CSR—Kant's categorical imperative, Mill's utilitarianism, and Rawls's theory of justice—provide us with a robust ethical framework for our corporate actions. They remind us that our responsibility extends beyond profits to encompass the well-being of all our stakeholders and the broader society."

With a renewed sense of purpose and ethical clarity, the executives at Apex Global Consulting prepared to integrate these philosophical principles into their CSR strategies, knowing that they held the key to building a more responsible and impactful organization.

The Business Case for CSR

Having explored the philosophical foundations of Corporate Social Responsibility (CSR), Michael sensed the growing curiosity among the executives. He knew the next step was crucial: demonstrating how these principles translate into tangible business benefits. The room was charged with anticipation as Michael prepared to present the business case for CSR.

"Now that we've examined the philosophical underpinnings of CSR," Michael began, his voice firm and engaging, "let's shift our focus to the **business case for CSR**. Understanding the tangible benefits can help us integrate these principles into our strategic goals more effectively."

He clicked the remote, and the screen illuminated with the title: **"The Business Case for CSR."**

"Our journey begins with **enhanced brand reputation and loyalty**," Michael continued, gesturing towards the screen. "Companies that engage in CSR activities are often viewed more favorably by consumers. They are seen as responsible, ethical, and trustworthy."

The screen transitioned to an image of a diverse group of happy customers and employees wearing branded apparel. "For example, when consumers see that a company is committed to environmental sustainability, they are more likely to support and remain loyal to that brand. This not only helps in retaining customers but also attracts new ones who value ethical practices."

Michael continued, "Consider the case of **Unilever**. By committing to sustainable sourcing and reducing environmental impact, Unilever has not only boosted its brand reputation but also seen increased sales growth in its sustainable product lines."

The executives nodded, acknowledging the direct correlation between CSR and brand loyalty.

"Next," Michael said, clicking to the next slide, "we delve into **employee engagement and retention**. CSR initiatives can significantly boost employee morale and loyalty."

The screen displayed images of employees participating in community service projects and corporate wellness programs. "When employees feel that their company is making a positive impact on society, they are more likely to be engaged and committed to their work. This leads to higher productivity and reduced turnover."

Michael continued, "For instance, **Patagonia** not only focuses on environmental sustainability but also encourages employees to volunteer for environmental causes, offering paid time off for activism. This has led to a highly motivated and loyal workforce."

The executives leaned forward, considering how to foster similar levels of engagement and loyalty within their own teams.

"Our journey also involves **risk management**," Michael said, bringing up an image of a company navigating through turbulent waters. "Companies that ignore their social responsibilities can face significant risks, including legal issues, boycotts, and reputational damage."

The screen transitioned to visuals of news headlines highlighting companies facing backlash for unethical practices. "By proactively addressing social and environmental issues, companies can mitigate these risks and protect their reputation. This not only prevents potential crises but also positions the company as a leader in responsible business practices."

Michael explained, "For example, **Johnson & Johnson** has implemented rigorous safety and quality standards in response to past controversies. This proactive approach has helped restore and maintain consumer trust."

He paused, allowing the significance of risk management to resonate with the team. "Another key benefit is **innovation and competitive advantage**," Michael said, clicking to the next slide. "CSR can drive innovation by encouraging companies to develop sustainable products and practices."

The screen displayed images of innovative products and sustainable technologies. "Companies like **Tesla** have revolutionized the automotive industry by focusing on electric vehicles and renewable energy solutions. This not only addresses environmental concerns but also provides a significant competitive advantage."

Michael continued, "By investing in sustainable innovation, companies can differentiate themselves in the market and attract environmentally conscious consumers."

The executives nodded thoughtfully, acknowledging the potential for CSR to drive innovation.

"In conclusion," Michael said, turning off the projector and facing his team, "the business case for CSR is compelling. Enhanced brand reputation, increased employee engagement, effective risk management, and driving innovation are just a few of the tangible benefits. By integrating CSR into our business strategies, we not only fulfill our ethical responsibilities but also achieve sustainable business success."

With a renewed sense of purpose and a clear understanding of the business benefits, the executives at Apex Global Consulting prepared to embed CSR principles into their strategic planning, knowing that they held the key to building a more responsible and prosperous organization.

Ethical Theories Applied to CSR

The executives at Apex Global Consulting were already captivated by the compelling business case for Corporate Social Responsibility (CSR). Michael could see their excitement and readiness to dive deeper. It was time to bridge the gap between theory and practice by exploring how ethical theories could be directly applied to CSR initiatives.

"Now that we've seen the tangible benefits of CSR," Michael began, his voice steady and insightful, "let's delve into how **ethical theories can be applied to CSR**. This will provide us with a robust framework to guide our CSR strategies and initiatives."

He clicked the remote, and the screen illuminated with the title: **"Ethical Theories Applied to CSR."**

"Our first theory is **Utilitarianism**," Michael continued, gesturing towards the screen. "As you know, utilitarianism focuses on maximizing overall happiness and minimizing suffering. This principle can be directly applied to our CSR efforts."

The screen transitioned to an image of a community outreach program with happy children and volunteers. "When planning CSR initiatives, we should evaluate the potential impact of our actions on all stakeholders. This means considering how our activities can create the greatest good for the greatest number of people."

Michael continued, "For example, **Google** has various CSR programs aimed at improving education, reducing carbon footprints, and supporting local communities. By prioritizing projects that offer widespread benefits, Google ensures its CSR efforts maximize positive impact."

The executives nodded, visualizing how utilitarian principles could guide their own CSR initiatives.

"Next," Michael said, clicking to the next slide, "we explore **Kantian Ethics**. Kant's categorical imperative challenges us to act according to principles that we would want to become universal laws."

The screen displayed images of a company implementing fair labor practices. "In the context of CSR, this means adopting practices that respect the dignity and rights of all individuals involved, from employees to suppliers to community members."

Michael explained, "For instance, **Ben & Jerry's** has built its brand on ethical sourcing, fair trade practices, and social justice. Their commitment to these principles ensures that their business practices can be universally accepted and respected."

The executives leaned forward, considering how to integrate Kantian ethics into their CSR policies.

"Our journey also involves **Virtue Ethics**," Michael said, bringing up an image of a corporate leader embodying integrity and responsibility. "Virtue ethics focuses on the character and virtues of individuals and organizations."

The screen transitioned to visuals of corporate leaders engaging in community service. "CSR initiatives guided by virtue ethics emphasize the importance of virtues like honesty, integrity, and responsibility. This approach encourages us to build a corporate culture that promotes ethical behavior at all levels."

Michael continued, "A notable example is **Patagonia**, whose leaders and employees embody a commitment to environmental stewardship and social responsibility. By fostering a culture of virtue, Patagonia ensures that its CSR efforts are genuine and impactful."

The executives nodded thoughtfully, recognizing the importance of cultivating virtues within their organization.

"In conclusion," Michael said, turning off the projector and facing his team, "applying ethical theories to CSR provides us with a strong foundation for our initiatives. Utilitarianism helps us maximize positive impact, Kantian ethics ensures our practices are universally justifiable, and virtue ethics guides us to cultivate ethical behavior within our organization."

With a renewed sense of ethical clarity and direction, the executives at Apex Global Consulting prepared to integrate these ethical theories into their CSR strategies, knowing that they held the key to creating a more responsible and principled organization.

Case Studies of Successful CSR Initiatives

The air in the room was thick with anticipation as Michael transitioned to the next segment of the discussion. Having established the ethical foundations and business rationale for Corporate Social Responsibility (CSR), it was time to bring these concepts to life through real-world examples. The executives were eager to see how successful companies had implemented CSR initiatives effectively.

"Now, let's examine some **case studies of successful CSR initiatives**," Michael announced, his voice filled with enthusiasm. "These examples will illustrate how various organizations have applied the principles we've discussed and the tangible impact they've achieved."

He clicked the remote, and the screen illuminated with the title: **"Case Studies of Successful CSR Initiatives."**

"Our first case study is **Unilever**," Michael began, as the screen displayed images of Unilever's diverse product range and sustainability efforts. "Unilever's Sustainable Living Plan aims to decouple the company's growth from its environmental footprint while increasing its positive social impact."

The screen transitioned to visuals of Unilever's projects, including sustainable sourcing of raw materials and community support initiatives. "Unilever has committed to sourcing 100% of its agricultural raw materials sustainably. They've also focused on improving health and well-being for more than a billion people and enhancing the livelihoods of millions of people across their value chain."

Michael continued, "By integrating sustainability into their core business strategy, Unilever has not only reduced costs and risks but also strengthened its brand and consumer loyalty."

The executives nodded, impressed by the scale and scope of Unilever's CSR efforts.

"Next, let's look at **Microsoft**," Michael said, clicking to the next slide. "Microsoft has made significant strides in corporate social responsibility, particularly in the areas of environmental sustainability and community empowerment."

The screen displayed images of Microsoft's renewable energy projects and digital inclusion programs. "Microsoft has committed to becoming carbon negative by 2030. They're also investing in initiatives that provide digital skills to underserved communities, helping to bridge the digital divide."

Michael explained, "Through these efforts, Microsoft not

only addresses pressing global issues but also fosters innovation and opens up new markets, demonstrating how CSR can drive business growth."

The executives leaned forward, eager to learn more about the practical applications of CSR.

"Our journey also takes us to **TOMS Shoes**," Michael said, bringing up an image of TOMS' iconic shoes and their social impact initiatives. "TOMS has built its brand on a simple yet powerful business model: for every pair of shoes sold, they donate a pair to a child in need."

The screen transitioned to visuals of children receiving shoes and other community support programs. "This 'One for One' model has provided millions of shoes to children worldwide, improving health and educational outcomes. TOMS has also expanded its impact by supporting safe water, eye care, and bullying prevention programs."

Michael continued, "By embedding social impact into their business model, TOMS has created a strong, loyal customer base that values purpose-driven brands."

The executives nodded thoughtfully, recognizing the potential for integrating social impact into their own business models.

"Another inspiring example is **IKEA**," Michael said, clicking to the next slide. "IKEA's People & Planet Positive strategy focuses on sustainability throughout its entire value chain."

The screen displayed images of IKEA's sustainable products and renewable energy initiatives. "IKEA aims to use only renewable and recycled materials in its products by 2030. They've also invested heavily in renewable energy, generating more energy than they consume."

Michael explained, "IKEA's commitment to sustainability

not only reduces its environmental impact but also drives innovation and strengthens its brand appeal."

He paused, letting the significance of these case studies sink in. "In conclusion," Michael said, turning off the projector and facing his team, "these case studies of Unilever, Microsoft, TOMS Shoes, and IKEA demonstrate that successful CSR initiatives can create substantial positive impacts while driving business success. By learning from these examples, we can develop our own CSR strategies that align with our values and business goals."

With a renewed sense of inspiration and practical insights, the executives at Apex Global Consulting prepared to craft their own CSR initiatives, knowing that they held the key to building a more sustainable and socially responsible organization.

Integrating CSR into Corporate Strategy

As the executives at Apex Global Consulting absorbed the lessons from the inspiring case studies of successful CSR initiatives, Michael sensed their eagerness to understand how to implement similar strategies within their own organization. It was time to delve into the crucial aspect of integrating CSR into corporate strategy.

"Now that we've explored the impact of CSR initiatives, let's discuss how to **integrate CSR into corporate strategy**," Michael announced, his voice resonating with purpose. "By aligning CSR with our core business objectives, we can maximize its impact and ensure sustainability."

He clicked the remote, and the screen illuminated with the title: **"Integrating CSR into Corporate Strategy."**

"Our journey begins with **strategic alignment**," Michael continued, gesturing towards the screen. "CSR initiatives must be integrated seamlessly into our overall business strategy. This means identifying areas where CSR efforts can create shared value for both the company and society."

The screen transitioned to visuals of a strategic planning session, with executives discussing CSR goals alongside financial targets. "For example, if one of our strategic goals is to expand into emerging markets, we can incorporate CSR initiatives that address local community needs and environmental sustainability. This not only enhances our brand reputation but also fosters goodwill and support from local stakeholders."

Michael continued, "By embedding CSR into our strategic planning process, we ensure that it becomes an integral part of our decision-making and resource allocation."

The executives nodded, recognizing the importance of strategic alignment in driving meaningful CSR outcomes.

"Next," Michael said, clicking to the next slide, "we must **engage stakeholders** effectively. Successful CSR initiatives require collaboration and buy-in from various stakeholders, including employees, customers, investors, and local communities."

The screen displayed images of diverse stakeholders engaging in dialogue and collaboration. "By actively involving stakeholders in the development and implementation of CSR strategies, we gain valuable insights, build trust, and create shared ownership over our initiatives."

Michael explained, "For instance, **Nike** engages with suppliers, workers, and NGOs to address labor rights and environmental sustainability issues in its supply chain. This collaborative approach not only improves working conditions but also enhances supply chain transparency and efficiency."

The executives leaned forward, considering how to engage their own stakeholders in CSR efforts.

"Our journey also involves **performance measurement and reporting**," Michael said, bringing up an image of a CSR dashboard displaying key metrics. "To ensure accountability and drive continuous improvement, we must establish clear performance metrics and mechanisms for tracking and reporting CSR outcomes."

The screen transitioned to visuals of CSR reports and impact assessments. "Regularly measuring and reporting on CSR performance allows us to assess the effectiveness of our initiatives, identify areas for improvement, and communicate our progress transparently to stakeholders."

Michael continued, "For example, **Walmart** publishes an annual Global Responsibility Report, highlighting its progress and challenges in areas such as environmental sustainability, supply chain ethics, and community engagement."

He paused, letting the significance of performance measurement sink in. "In conclusion," Michael said, turning off the projector and facing his team, "integrating CSR into our corporate strategy requires strategic alignment, stakeholder engagement, and robust performance measurement. By embedding CSR into our DNA, we can create long-term value for our company, society, and the environment."

With a renewed sense of purpose and practical guidance, the executives at Apex Global Consulting prepared to integrate CSR seamlessly into their corporate strategy, knowing that they held the key to building a more sustainable and socially responsible organization.

Measuring and Reporting CSR Efforts

As the discussion on integrating CSR into corporate strategy reached its pinnacle, Michael prepared to shed light on the critical aspect of measuring and reporting CSR efforts. The executives at Apex Global Consulting were eager to understand how to track the impact of their initiatives and communicate their progress effectively.

"Now, let's explore the importance of **measuring and reporting CSR efforts**," Michael announced, his voice filled with gravitas. "By quantifying our impact and sharing our progress transparently, we can demonstrate accountability and inspire confidence among stakeholders."

He clicked the remote, and the screen illuminated with the title: **"Measuring and Reporting CSR Efforts."**

"Our journey begins with **establishing clear metrics**," Michael continued, gesturing towards the screen. "To effectively measure the impact of our CSR initiatives, we must identify key performance indicators (KPIs) that align with our strategic objectives and stakeholder expectations."

The screen transitioned to visuals of a CSR dashboard displaying various KPIs, such as carbon emissions reduction, employee volunteer hours, and community engagement metrics. "For example, if our CSR goal is to reduce our carbon footprint, we can track metrics such as energy consumption, waste generation, and greenhouse gas emissions. These metrics provide tangible data points to evaluate our progress over time."

Michael explained, "By establishing clear metrics, we ensure that our CSR efforts are measurable, actionable, and aligned with our overall objectives."

The executives nodded, recognizing the importance of quantifying their CSR impact.

"Next," Michael said, clicking to the next slide, "we must **implement robust reporting mechanisms**. Transparent reporting is essential for communicating our CSR efforts to stakeholders and fostering trust and credibility."

The screen displayed images of CSR reports and stakeholder engagement sessions. "We can create annual CSR reports that provide a comprehensive overview of our initiatives, progress, and challenges. These reports should include qualitative and quantitative data, case studies, and testimonials to illustrate our impact and commitment to corporate responsibility."

Michael continued, "In addition to formal reports, we can leverage digital platforms, social media, and stakeholder engagement sessions to communicate our CSR efforts in real-time and gather feedback from stakeholders."

The executives leaned forward, eager to learn how to effectively communicate their CSR efforts.

"Our journey also involves **third-party verification and certification**," Michael said, bringing up an image of a CSR certification seal. "To enhance credibility and transparency, we can seek third-party verification and certification for our CSR initiatives."

The screen transitioned to visuals of reputable certification bodies and their criteria for CSR certification. "Certifications such as B Corp, ISO 26000, and GRI Standards provide independent validation of our CSR practices and adherence to international standards. These certifications serve as a stamp of approval, assuring stakeholders of our commitment to responsible business practices."

Michael explained, "By obtaining third-party verification

and certification, we demonstrate accountability and differentiate ourselves as leaders in corporate responsibility."

He paused, letting the significance of third-party verification sink in. "In conclusion," Michael said, turning off the projector and facing his team, "measuring and reporting CSR efforts is essential for demonstrating accountability, transparency, and credibility. By establishing clear metrics, implementing robust reporting mechanisms, and seeking third-party verification, we can effectively communicate our CSR impact and inspire trust among stakeholders."

With a renewed commitment to transparency and accountability, the executives at Apex Global Consulting prepared to implement comprehensive measurement and reporting mechanisms for their CSR initiatives, knowing that they held the key to building a more sustainable and socially responsible organization.

Chapter 8: Sustainability and Ethical Management

Philosophical Foundations of Sustainability

As the executives at Apex Global Consulting gathered for their next meeting, anticipation filled the room. Michael sensed the eagerness to explore the intersection of sustainability and ethical management—the cornerstone of their organization's values. It was time to delve into the philosophical foundations that underpin sustainable business practices.

"Today, we embark on a journey to explore **Sustainability and Ethical Management**," Michael announced, his voice resonating with conviction. "At the heart of our discussion lies the philosophical foundations that guide our approach to sustainability."

He clicked the remote, and the screen illuminated with the title: **"Sustainability and Ethical Management."**

"Our journey begins with the **philosophical foundations of sustainability**," Michael continued, gesturing towards the screen. "Sustainability is more than just a business strategy; it's a moral imperative rooted in deep philosophical principles."

The screen transitioned to images of pristine natural landscapes and diverse ecosystems. "Philosophers such as **Aldo Leopold** and **Rachel Carson** have emphasized the interconnectedness of all life forms and the inherent value of nature. Their works laid the groundwork for modern environmental ethics, highlighting the moral responsibility to protect and preserve the environment for future generations."

Michael explained, "At its core, sustainability embodies the principles of **intergenerational equity, ecological integrity**, and **social justice**. It challenges us to adopt a holistic perspective that considers the long-term consequences of our actions on the planet and its inhabitants."

The executives nodded, recognizing the profound ethical implications of sustainability.

"Next," Michael said, clicking to the next slide, "we explore the concept of **deep ecology**. Deep ecology advocates for a radical shift in human consciousness, from viewing ourselves as separate from nature to recognizing our interconnectedness with all living beings."

The screen displayed images of activists protesting deforestation and advocating for conservation. "Deep ecology calls for a fundamental reevaluation of our values and priorities, placing intrinsic value on all life forms and ecosystems. This philosophical perspective challenges us to embrace humility, compassion, and ecological wisdom in our interactions with the natural world."

Michael continued, "By embracing deep ecology principles, we can cultivate a profound sense of reverence and stewardship towards the Earth, guiding our sustainable business practices."

The executives leaned forward, captivated by the profound

insights of deep ecology.

"Our journey also involves **eco-feminism**," Michael said, bringing up an image of women leading environmental movements. "Eco-feminism explores the intersectionality of gender and environmental issues, recognizing the disproportionate impact of environmental degradation on women and marginalized communities."

The screen transitioned to visuals of women advocating for environmental justice and sustainable development. "Eco-feminism emphasizes the need for a holistic and inclusive approach to sustainability that addresses social inequalities and promotes gender equality. By amplifying the voices of women and indigenous peoples, we can create more resilient and equitable societies."

Michael explained, "By integrating eco-feminist principles into our sustainability efforts, we can foster greater diversity, inclusivity, and resilience within our organization and society at large."

He paused, allowing the significance of these philosophical foundations to resonate with the team. "In conclusion," Michael said, turning off the projector and facing his team, "the philosophical foundations of sustainability provide us with a moral compass to navigate the complexities of ethical management. By embracing principles such as intergenerational equity, ecological integrity, and social justice, we can build a more sustainable and equitable future for all."

With a renewed sense of purpose and ethical clarity, the executives at Apex Global Consulting prepared to integrate these philosophical principles into their sustainability initiatives, knowing that they held the key to building a more resilient and ethical organization.

Ethics of Environmental Stewardship

As the discussion on sustainability and ethical management continued, Michael shifted the focus towards the ethics of environmental stewardship, a pivotal aspect of their organization's commitment to responsible business practices. The executives leaned in, eager to delve deeper into the moral imperatives surrounding environmental conservation.

"Now, let's explore the **ethics of environmental stewardship**," Michael announced, his voice carrying a sense of reverence for the natural world. "At the heart of sustainable business practices lies our ethical responsibility to protect and preserve the environment for future generations."

He clicked the remote, and the screen illuminated with the title: **"Ethics of Environmental Stewardship."**

"Our journey begins with the recognition that we are stewards of the Earth," Michael continued, gesturing towards the screen. "As custodians of this planet, we have a moral obligation to act in ways that safeguard the integrity of our ecosystems and mitigate the impact of human activities on the environment."

The screen transitioned to images of deforestation, pollution, and wildlife habitats threatened by human encroachment. "The ethics of environmental stewardship compel us to consider the intrinsic value of nature and the rights of non-human beings to exist and thrive in their natural habitats."

Michael explained, "Environmental stewardship requires us to adopt a mindset of humility, reverence, and responsibility towards the Earth. It challenges us to recognize the interconnectedness of all life forms and the delicate balance that sustains our planet's ecosystems."

The executives nodded, understanding the profound ethical implications of their role as environmental stewards.

"Next," Michael said, clicking to the next slide, "we explore the principle of **sustainability ethics**. Sustainability ethics emphasizes the need to prioritize long-term ecological health and well-being over short-term economic gain."

The screen displayed images of renewable energy projects, sustainable agriculture practices, and conservation efforts. "Sustainability ethics calls for a shift away from exploitative and extractive practices towards regenerative and restorative approaches that ensure the continued vitality of our planet."

Michael continued, "By embracing sustainability ethics, we can create win-win solutions that benefit both people and the planet. This requires innovative thinking, collaboration, and a willingness to challenge the status quo."

The executives leaned forward, inspired by the vision of a sustainable future guided by ethical principles.

"Our journey also involves **environmental justice**," Michael said, bringing up an image of communities impacted by environmental degradation. "Environmental justice recognizes that marginalized communities often bear the brunt of environmental pollution and resource depletion, exacerbating social inequalities."

The screen transitioned to visuals of activists advocating for environmental justice and equitable access to clean air, water, and land. "Environmental justice demands that we address the root causes of environmental injustice and ensure that all individuals, regardless of race, ethnicity, or socioeconomic status, have equal protection under environmental laws and regulations."

Michael explained, "By promoting environmental justice,

we can create more inclusive and resilient communities that prioritize the well-being of all their members."

He paused, allowing the significance of environmental stewardship ethics to sink in. "In conclusion," Michael said, turning off the projector and facing his team, "the ethics of environmental stewardship challenge us to embrace our role as guardians of the Earth and act with integrity, compassion, and foresight. By integrating sustainability ethics and promoting environmental justice, we can create a more sustainable and equitable world for current and future generations."

With a renewed sense of purpose and commitment to environmental stewardship, the executives at Apex Global Consulting prepared to elevate their sustainability efforts, knowing that they held the key to building a more resilient and ethical organization.

Sustainable Business Practices

As the executives at Apex Global Consulting continued their exploration of sustainability and ethical management, Michael shifted the focus towards the practical implementation of sustainable business practices. The room buzzed with anticipation as they prepared to uncover actionable strategies for integrating sustainability into their day-to-day operations.

"Now, let's turn our attention to **sustainable business practices**," Michael announced, his voice infused with determination. "To truly embody our commitment to environmental stewardship, we must translate our ethical principles into tangible actions that drive positive change."

He clicked the remote, and the screen illuminated with the

title: "**Sustainable Business Practices.**"

"Our journey begins with the recognition that sustainability must be integrated into every aspect of our organization," Michael continued, gesturing towards the screen. "From procurement and production to marketing and distribution, sustainable business practices require a holistic approach that considers the environmental, social, and economic impacts of our operations."

The screen transitioned to images of energy-efficient buildings, waste reduction initiatives, and eco-friendly packaging designs. "Sustainable business practices encompass a wide range of strategies, including resource conservation, waste minimization, renewable energy adoption, and supply chain transparency."

Michael explained, "By adopting sustainable business practices, we can reduce our environmental footprint, enhance operational efficiency, and create value for our stakeholders."

The executives nodded, recognizing the transformative potential of sustainable business practices.

"Next," Michael said, clicking to the next slide, "we explore the concept of **circular economy**. A circular economy aims to minimize waste and maximize resource efficiency by designing products, processes, and systems that prioritize reuse, recycling, and regeneration."

The screen displayed images of closed-loop supply chains, remanufacturing facilities, and product lifecycle assessments. "In a circular economy, waste becomes a valuable resource, and products are designed with end-of-life considerations in mind. This shift from a linear 'take-make-dispose' model to a circular 'reduce-reuse-recycle' model enables us to decouple economic growth from resource consumption and environmental degradation."

Michael continued, "By embracing the principles of the circular economy, we can create resilient and regenerative business models that contribute to a more sustainable future."

The executives leaned forward, inspired by the potential of the circular economy to transform their industry.

"Our journey also involves **sustainable innovation**," Michael said, bringing up an image of a research and development laboratory. "Sustainable innovation involves the development of new products, services, and technologies that address environmental and social challenges while delivering value to customers and shareholders."

The screen transitioned to visuals of sustainable innovations, such as renewable energy technologies, green building materials, and zero-waste packaging solutions. "Sustainable innovation requires creativity, collaboration, and a willingness to challenge conventional thinking. By investing in research and development efforts that prioritize sustainability, we can drive positive change and unlock new opportunities for growth and differentiation."

Michael explained, "By integrating sustainable innovation into our business strategy, we can foster a culture of continuous improvement and resilience that positions us as leaders in our industry."

He paused, allowing the significance of sustainable business practices to sink in. "In conclusion," Michael said, turning off the projector and facing his team, "sustainable business practices are essential for realizing our vision of environmental stewardship and ethical management. By embracing the principles of the circular economy, fostering sustainable innovation, and integrating sustainability into every aspect of our operations, we can build a more resilient, responsible, and prosperous organization."

With a renewed sense of purpose and determination, the executives at Apex Global Consulting prepared to implement sustainable business practices that would not only benefit their company but also contribute to a more sustainable and equitable world for future generations.

Case Studies in Corporate Sustainability

As the executives at Apex Global Consulting delved deeper into the realm of sustainable business practices, Michael recognized the power of real-world examples to illustrate the transformative potential of corporate sustainability. With eager anticipation, the team awaited the unveiling of case studies showcasing successful implementations of sustainable initiatives.

"Now, let's delve into **case studies in corporate sustainability**," Michael announced, his voice brimming with excitement. "These examples will demonstrate how leading organizations have embraced sustainability as a core value and achieved remarkable results."

He clicked the remote, and the screen illuminated with the title: **"Case Studies in Corporate Sustainability."**

"Our journey begins with **Interface, Inc.**," Michael continued, gesturing towards the screen. "Interface, a global leader in modular flooring, has been at the forefront of sustainable business practices for decades."

The screen transitioned to images of Interface's sustainable initiatives, including its Mission Zero commitment to eliminate its negative environmental impact by 2020. "Interface's journey towards sustainability began with the vision of its founder, Ray Anderson, who challenged the company to reimagine its business model in harmony with nature."

Michael explained, "Through innovative product design, resource conservation efforts, and renewable energy investments, Interface has reduced its carbon footprint, water usage, and waste generation while increasing operational efficiency and customer satisfaction."

The executives nodded, impressed by Interface's commitment to sustainability and its tangible results.

"Next," Michael said, clicking to the next slide, "we have **Patagonia**. Patagonia, an outdoor apparel company, has become synonymous with environmental activism and corporate responsibility."

The screen displayed images of Patagonia's sustainable practices, including its commitment to using recycled materials, fair labor practices, and advocacy for environmental protection. "Patagonia's founder, Yvon Chouinard, has embedded sustainability into the company's DNA, prioritizing environmental and social responsibility over short-term profits."

Michael continued, "Patagonia's sustainable business practices have not only earned it loyal customers but also positioned it as a leader in the outdoor industry and a powerful advocate for environmental conservation."

The executives leaned forward, inspired by Patagonia's holistic approach to sustainability.

"Our journey also takes us to **Unilever**," Michael said, bringing up an image of Unilever's Sustainable Living Plan. "Unilever, a multinational consumer goods company, has made sustainability a cornerstone of its business strategy."

The screen transitioned to visuals of Unilever's sustainable initiatives, including its commitments to sustainable sourcing, waste reduction, and social impact. "Unilever's Sustainable Living Plan aims to improve the health and well-being of billions of people, reduce its environmental footprint, and enhance livelihoods across its value chain."

Michael explained, "Through initiatives such as the Dove Self-Esteem Project and the Sustainable Agriculture Code, Unilever is demonstrating how businesses can drive positive social and environmental change while delivering long-term value to shareholders."

He paused, allowing the significance of these case studies to resonate with the team. "In conclusion," Michael said, turning off the projector and facing his team, "these case studies in corporate sustainability serve as beacons of inspiration, demonstrating the transformative power of sustainability as a driver of innovation, resilience, and value creation. By learning from their successes and challenges, we can chart our own path towards a more sustainable and prosperous future."

With a renewed sense of purpose and determination, the executives at Apex Global Consulting prepared to draw upon the lessons of these case studies to accelerate their own journey towards corporate sustainability, knowing that they held the key to building a more resilient and responsible organization.

The Role of Leadership in Promoting Sustainability

As the executives at Apex Global Consulting delved deeper into the complexities of corporate sustainability, Michael recognized the pivotal role of leadership in driving meaningful change within their organization. With a sense of urgency, he prepared to unveil the critical importance of leadership in promoting sustainability and ethical management.

"Now, let's explore **the role of leadership in promoting sustainability**," Michael announced, his voice infused with conviction. "Leadership is not just about setting goals and making decisions—it's about inspiring others to embrace a shared vision and take action towards a better future."

He clicked the remote, and the screen illuminated with the title: **"The Role of Leadership in Promoting Sustainability."**

"Our journey begins with the recognition that **leadership sets the tone** for an organization's sustainability efforts," Michael continued, gesturing towards the screen. "Effective leaders lead by example, demonstrating a genuine commitment to sustainability in their words and actions."

The screen transitioned to images of visionary leaders championing sustainability initiatives, from reducing carbon emissions to fostering diversity and inclusion. "Leaders who prioritize sustainability inspire trust, accountability, and innovation among their teams. They create a culture where sustainability is not just a checkbox but a fundamental value that guides decision-making at every level of the organization."

Michael explained, "By embodying the principles of sustainability in their leadership style, leaders can unleash the full potential of their teams and drive transformative change that benefits both the organization and society."

The executives nodded, recognizing the profound impact of leadership on organizational culture and performance.

"Next," Michael said, clicking to the next slide, "we explore the concept of **transformational leadership**. Transformational leaders inspire and empower others to achieve their full potential, fostering a culture of innovation, collaboration, and continuous improvement."

The screen displayed images of transformational leaders leading by example, communicating a compelling vision, and empowering their teams to overcome challenges and seize opportunities. "Transformational leaders embrace sustainability as a strategic imperative, aligning organizational goals with environmental and social priorities. They challenge the status quo, break down silos, and cultivate a sense of purpose and belonging among their teams."

Michael continued, "By fostering a culture of sustainability and empowering employees to contribute their ideas and talents, transformational leaders can drive meaningful progress towards a more sustainable and equitable future."

The executives leaned forward, inspired by the vision of leadership as a catalyst for positive change.

"Our journey also involves **collaborative leadership**," Michael said, bringing up an image of leaders collaborating across sectors to address global challenges. "Collaborative leaders recognize that sustainability is not a solo endeavor but a collective responsibility that requires partnership and collaboration across stakeholders."

The screen transitioned to visuals of collaborative initiatives, such as public-private partnerships, industry coalitions, and multi-stakeholder platforms. "Collaborative leaders leverage their networks, influence, and resources to forge partnerships, build consensus, and drive systemic change. They recognize the interconnectedness of global challenges and the need for collective action to address them."

Michael explained, "By fostering collaboration and collective impact, leaders can amplify the reach and effectiveness of their sustainability efforts, accelerating progress towards shared goals and objectives."

He paused, allowing the significance of leadership in promoting sustainability to sink in. "In conclusion," Michael said, turning off the projector and facing his team, "the role of leadership in promoting sustainability is paramount. By leading by example, embracing transformational and collaborative leadership approaches, leaders can inspire others to join them on the journey towards a more sustainable and prosperous future."

With a renewed sense of purpose and determination, the executives at Apex Global Consulting prepared to step into their roles as sustainability leaders, knowing that they held the key to unlocking a brighter, more sustainable future for their organization and society.

Tools and Frameworks for Sustainable Management

As the executives at Apex Global Consulting delved deeper into their exploration of sustainability and ethical management, Michael sensed their eagerness to equip themselves with practical tools and frameworks to navigate the complexities of sustainable management. With a sense of purpose, he prepared to unveil a suite of resources that would empower them to drive positive change within their organization.

"Now, let's turn our attention to **tools and frameworks for sustainable management**," Michael announced, his voice infused with determination. "These resources will serve as guiding lights on our journey towards integrating sustainability into every aspect of our organization."

He clicked the remote, and the screen illuminated with the

title: **"Tools and Frameworks for Sustainable Management."**

"Our journey begins with the recognition that **measurement is key**," Michael continued, gesturing towards the screen. "To effectively manage sustainability, we must first understand where we stand and where we aspire to be. This requires robust measurement and tracking of key performance indicators (KPIs) related to environmental, social, and governance (ESG) factors."

The screen transitioned to images of sustainability dashboards, reporting frameworks, and data analytics tools. "Tools such as sustainability scorecards, life cycle assessments, and carbon footprint calculators enable us to quantify our environmental impact, identify areas for improvement, and track progress towards our sustainability goals."

Michael explained, "By leveraging these measurement tools, we can make informed decisions, allocate resources effectively, and drive continuous improvement in our sustainability performance."

The executives nodded, recognizing the importance of data-driven decision-making in sustainable management.

"Next," Michael said, clicking to the next slide, "we explore the concept of **sustainability frameworks**. Sustainability frameworks provide structured approaches for integrating sustainability into business strategy, operations, and decision-making processes."

The screen displayed images of popular sustainability frameworks, such as the Global Reporting Initiative (GRI) Standards, the UN Sustainable Development Goals (SDGs), and the Triple Bottom Line (TBL) approach. "These frameworks help organizations define their sustainability priorities, set goals and targets, and communicate their progress transparently to stakeholders."

Michael continued, "By aligning our sustainability efforts with recognized frameworks, we can ensure consistency, comparability, and credibility in our reporting and disclosure practices."

The executives leaned forward, eager to learn how to effectively apply these frameworks within their organization.

"Our journey also involves **stakeholder engagement tools**," Michael said, bringing up an image of a stakeholder mapping exercise. "Effective stakeholder engagement is essential for understanding stakeholder expectations, building trust, and fostering collaboration towards shared sustainability goals."

The screen transitioned to visuals of stakeholder engagement platforms, materiality assessments, and multi-stakeholder dialogues. "Tools such as stakeholder mapping exercises, materiality assessments, and online engagement platforms enable us to identify key stakeholders, prioritize their concerns, and develop tailored strategies for engagement."

Michael explained, "By engaging stakeholders in meaningful dialogue and co-creation processes, we can build consensus, address complex challenges, and generate shared value for all parties involved."

He paused, allowing the significance of these tools and frameworks to sink in. "In conclusion," Michael said, turning off the projector and facing his team, "tools and frameworks for sustainable management provide us with the roadmap and navigational tools we need to steer our organization towards a more sustainable and prosperous future. By leveraging these resources effectively, we can build resilience, drive innovation, and create long-term value for our company, society, and the planet."

With a renewed sense of purpose and armed with practical tools and frameworks, the executives at Apex Global Consulting prepared to embark on their sustainability journey, knowing that they held the key to unlocking a brighter, more sustainable future for their organization and the world.

Chapter 9: The Philosophy of Work and Labor

Philosophical Perspectives on the Nature of Work

As the executives at Apex Global Consulting gathered for their next meeting, the topic at hand stirred curiosity and introspection. Michael, recognizing the significance of delving into the philosophical underpinnings of work and labor, prepared to lead them on a journey of contemplation and discovery.

"Today, we embark on a profound exploration of **The Philosophy of Work and Labor**," Michael announced, his voice resonating with a sense of anticipation. "At the heart of our discussion lies the fundamental question: What is the nature of work?"

He clicked the remote, and the screen illuminated with the title: **"The Philosophy of Work and Labor."**

"Our journey begins with the recognition that work is more than just a means of earning a living," Michael continued, gesturing towards the screen. "Work shapes our identities, influences our relationships, and contributes to our sense of purpose and fulfillment."

The screen transitioned to images of individuals engaged in various forms of work, from manual labor to creative endeavors. "Philosophers throughout history have contemplated the nature of work and its significance in human life. From Aristotle's notion of eudaimonia to Marx's theory of alienation, diverse perspectives have emerged, offering insights into the intrinsic value and meaning of work."

Michael explained, "At its essence, work is a manifestation of human creativity, ingenuity, and agency. It is through work that we transform raw materials into meaningful products, ideas into innovations, and aspirations into achievements."

The executives nodded, recognizing the profound impact of work on their lives and society as a whole.

"Next," Michael said, clicking to the next slide, "we explore the concept of **work as a social institution**. Work not only provides individuals with a means of sustenance but also serves as a cornerstone of social organization and cohesion."

The screen displayed images of workplaces, factories, and bustling marketplaces. "Work structures our daily routines, shapes our social interactions, and defines our roles and responsibilities within society. Whether through division of labor, specialization, or collaboration, work fosters interdependence and cooperation among individuals and communities."

Michael continued, "By examining work as a social institution, we gain insights into its role in shaping social norms, values, and power dynamics. From the guilds of medieval Europe to the factories of the Industrial Revolution, the evolution of work reflects broader changes in society and the economy."

The executives leaned forward, captivated by the historical

and sociological dimensions of work.

"Our journey also involves **existential perspectives on work**," Michael said, bringing up an image of individuals reflecting on the meaning of their work. "Existential philosophers such as Sartre and Camus have explored the existential dimensions of work, grappling with questions of authenticity, freedom, and responsibility."

The screen transitioned to visuals of individuals contemplating their work and its significance in their lives. "For existentialists, work represents more than just a means to an end—it is a vehicle for self-expression, self-actualization, and self-transcendence. Through work, we confront the fundamental questions of human existence and strive to create meaning in an often chaotic and absurd world."

Michael explained, "By embracing an existential perspective on work, we can cultivate a deeper sense of purpose, autonomy, and authenticity in our professional lives, enriching our experiences and relationships along the way."

He paused, allowing the significance of the philosophy of work and labor to resonate with the team. "In conclusion," Michael said, turning off the projector and facing his team, "the philosophy of work and labor invites us to reflect on the nature, purpose, and significance of our work. By embracing diverse philosophical perspectives, we can gain deeper insights into our roles as workers, leaders, and members of society, empowering us to create more meaningful and fulfilling work experiences for ourselves and others."

With a renewed sense of introspection and appreciation for the profound dimensions of work, the executives at Apex Global Consulting prepared to apply these philosophical insights to their professional endeavors, knowing that they held the key to unlocking greater meaning and fulfillment in their work and lives.

The Meaning and Purpose of Work

As the discussion on the philosophy of work and labor continued, Michael shifted the focus towards exploring the profound questions surrounding the meaning and purpose of work. The executives leaned in, eager to delve deeper into the existential dimensions of their professional lives.

"Now, let's delve into **the meaning and purpose of work**," Michael announced, his voice carrying a tone of contemplation. "At the core of our existence lies the quest to find meaning and purpose in our work, to understand why we do what we do."

He clicked the remote, and the screen illuminated with the title: **"The Meaning and Purpose of Work."**

"Our journey begins with the recognition that work is more than just a series of tasks to be completed," Michael continued, gesturing towards the screen. "It is a source of identity, fulfillment, and contribution to something greater than ourselves."

The screen transitioned to images of individuals engaged in various forms of work, their faces reflecting determination and purpose. "The meaning of work varies from person to person and is influenced by factors such as personal values, beliefs, and aspirations. For some, work is a means of survival, while for others, it is a calling, a vocation that aligns with their deepest passions and talents."

Michael explained, "At its essence, the meaning of work lies in the relationships we form, the impact we have on others, and the legacy we leave behind. Whether through creative expression, service to others, or pursuit of excellence, work becomes meaningful when it resonates with our values and contributes to our sense of fulfillment and purpose."

The executives nodded, reflecting on their own experiences and aspirations in relation to their work.

"Next," Michael said, clicking to the next slide, "we explore the concept of **work as a source of fulfillment**. Fulfillment in work comes from the sense of accomplishment, mastery, and autonomy it provides."

The screen displayed images of individuals immersed in their work, their faces radiating satisfaction and joy. "When work engages our skills, passions, and interests, it becomes more than just a job—it becomes a source of intrinsic motivation and satisfaction. This sense of fulfillment stems from the alignment between our work and our values, goals, and sense of self."

Michael continued, "By cultivating a deeper understanding of what truly matters to us and seeking opportunities to align our work with our values and aspirations, we can unlock greater fulfillment and meaning in our professional lives."

The executives leaned forward, captivated by the idea of finding fulfillment in their work.

"Our journey also involves **the pursuit of purpose**," Michael said, bringing up an image of individuals reflecting on their life's purpose. "Purpose in work goes beyond individual fulfillment—it is about contributing to something larger than ourselves, making a meaningful impact on the world around us."

The screen transitioned to visuals of individuals engaged in purpose-driven work, from social entrepreneurs to environmental activists. "When work is infused with purpose, it becomes a force for positive change, driving us to overcome obstacles, pursue excellence, and leave a lasting legacy. Purpose gives meaning to our efforts, inspiring us to strive for something greater than personal success or material gain."

Michael explained, "By aligning our work with our values, passions, and sense of purpose, we can create a more meaningful and fulfilling professional life, one that not only enriches our own lives but also uplifts others and contributes to the greater good."

He paused, allowing the significance of the meaning and purpose of work to resonate with the team. "In conclusion," Michael said, turning off the projector and facing his team, "the meaning and purpose of work invite us to reflect on what truly matters to us and why we do what we do. By embracing work as a source of fulfillment and pursuing purpose-driven endeavors, we can create more meaningful and fulfilling professional lives, ones that bring joy, satisfaction, and a sense of contribution to ourselves and others."

With a renewed sense of introspection and purpose, the executives at Apex Global Consulting prepared to apply these philosophical insights to their professional endeavors, knowing that they held the key to unlocking greater meaning and fulfillment in their work and lives.

Ethical Treatment of Employees

As the discussion on the philosophy of work and labor progressed, Michael turned the executives' attention towards the ethical treatment of employees, recognizing the profound impact it has on organizational culture and societal well-being.

CHAPTER 9: THE PHILOSOPHY OF WORK AND LABOR

The room grew somber as they prepared to confront the ethical dimensions of their roles as leaders.

"Now, let's explore **the ethical treatment of employees**," Michael announced, his voice carrying a weight of responsibility. "At the heart of our discussion lies the moral imperative to ensure the dignity, rights, and well-being of those who contribute their labor to our organization."

He clicked the remote, and the screen illuminated with the title: **"Ethical Treatment of Employees."**

"Our journey begins with the recognition that employees are not merely resources to be utilized but human beings deserving of respect, fairness, and compassion," Michael continued, gesturing towards the screen. "Ethical treatment of employees requires us to uphold their rights, promote their welfare, and create an environment where they can thrive and flourish."

The screen transitioned to images of diverse employees, their faces reflecting a range of emotions from joy to exhaustion. "From fair compensation and safe working conditions to opportunities for professional development and work-life balance, ethical treatment of employees encompasses a wide range of practices and policies that prioritize their dignity, well-being, and empowerment."

Michael explained, "At its essence, ethical treatment of employees is about fostering a culture of trust, transparency, and accountability within our organization. It is about recognizing the inherent value and worth of every individual and honoring their contributions with fairness, dignity, and respect."

The executives nodded solemnly, acknowledging the gravity of their responsibility towards their employees.

"Next," Michael said, clicking to the next slide, "we explore the concept of **equality and diversity in the workplace**. Ethical treatment of employees requires us to embrace diversity, equity, and inclusion as core values and principles."

The screen displayed images of diverse teams collaborating and celebrating their differences. "Equality and diversity in the workplace are not just moral imperatives—they are business imperatives. Diverse teams bring together different perspectives, experiences, and talents, fostering innovation, creativity, and resilience."

Michael continued, "By creating a culture of inclusivity and belonging, we can attract and retain top talent, enhance employee engagement and satisfaction, and drive better business outcomes."

The executives leaned forward, recognizing the importance of fostering a culture of diversity and inclusion.

"Our journey also involves **employee empowerment and participation**," Michael said, bringing up an image of employees engaged in decision-making processes. "Ethical treatment of employees requires us to empower them to voice their opinions, contribute their ideas, and participate in decision-making processes that affect their lives and livelihoods."

The screen transitioned to visuals of employees participating in team meetings, brainstorming sessions, and feedback forums. "Empowered employees are more engaged, motivated, and committed to their work and the organization. By involving them in decision-making processes, we not only tap into their expertise and insights but also foster a sense of ownership, accountability, and pride in their work."

Michael explained, "By empowering employees and fostering a culture of participation and collaboration, we can create a workplace where everyone feels valued, respected, and empowered to contribute their best."

He paused, allowing the significance of the ethical treatment of employees to resonate with the team. "In conclusion," Michael said, turning off the projector and facing his team, "the ethical treatment of employees is not just a moral imperative—it is a strategic imperative that drives organizational success and societal well-being. By upholding their rights, promoting their welfare, and empowering them to thrive, we can create a workplace that honors the dignity, worth, and humanity of every individual."

With a renewed sense of commitment to ethical leadership, the executives at Apex Global Consulting prepared to apply these principles to their interactions with employees, knowing that they held the key to fostering a culture of trust, respect, and empowerment within their organization.

Work-Life Balance and Its Philosophical Implications

As the discussion in the boardroom of Apex Global Consulting delved deeper into the philosophy of work and labor, Michael shifted the focus towards the intricate balance between work and life, recognizing its profound implications on the well-being and fulfillment of employees. The atmosphere in the room softened as they prepared to confront the philosophical dimensions of work-life balance.

"Now, let's explore **work-life balance and its philosophical implications**," Michael announced, his voice carrying a tone of empathy and understanding. "At the core of our discussion lies the recognition that our lives are not just defined by our work, but by the richness of our experiences, relationships, and pursuits outside of the office."

He clicked the remote, and the screen illuminated with the title: **"Work-Life Balance and Its Philosophical Implications."**

"Our journey begins with the acknowledgment that work-life balance is not just a matter of time management, but a reflection of our values, priorities, and aspirations," Michael continued, gesturing towards the screen. "It is about creating harmony between our professional and personal lives, so that we can lead fulfilling and meaningful lives both inside and outside the workplace."

The screen transitioned to images of individuals juggling the demands of work and life, their faces reflecting a range of emotions from stress to serenity. "Work-life balance is about more than just clocking in and out—it is about finding equilibrium between our professional responsibilities and our personal well-being, health, and happiness."

Michael explained, "At its essence, work-life balance is a philosophical concept that raises profound questions about the nature of work, the purpose of life, and the pursuit of happiness. It challenges us to reconsider our assumptions about success, productivity, and fulfillment, and to prioritize our well-being and relationships alongside our professional goals and ambitions."

The executives nodded in agreement, reflecting on their own struggles and aspirations for achieving balance in their lives.

"Next," Michael said, clicking to the next slide, "we explore the concept of **time vs. meaning**. In our pursuit of work-life balance, we often grapple with the tension between the time we spend working and the meaning we derive from our work."

CHAPTER 9: THE PHILOSOPHY OF WORK AND LABOR

The screen displayed images of individuals reflecting on the meaning of their work and its impact on their lives. "For some, work is a source of purpose, fulfillment, and identity, while for others, it is a means to an end, a necessary but mundane aspect of life. Balancing the demands of work and the desire for meaning requires us to reflect on our values, passions, and aspirations, and to align our work with our deeper sense of purpose and fulfillment."

Michael continued, "By redefining success not just in terms of professional achievements but also in terms of personal fulfillment, relationships, and well-being, we can create a more balanced and meaningful life for ourselves and those around us."

The executives leaned forward, captivated by the idea of finding meaning in their work and lives.

"Our journey also involves **the pursuit of authenticity**," Michael said, bringing up an image of individuals embracing their true selves in both work and life. "Work-life balance invites us to live authentically, to honor our values, passions, and priorities in both our professional and personal lives."

The screen transitioned to visuals of individuals living with integrity, purpose, and authenticity, both in and out of the workplace. "Authenticity requires us to be true to ourselves, to listen to our inner voice, and to make choices that align with our values and aspirations. By embracing authenticity, we can create a more integrated and harmonious life, where our work and our personal pursuits complement and enrich each other."

Michael explained, "By embracing work-life balance as a philosophical concept, we can transcend the limitations of conventional notions of success and productivity, and create lives that are rich in meaning, purpose, and fulfillment."

He paused, allowing the significance of work-life balance and its philosophical implications to resonate with the team. "In conclusion," Michael said, turning off the projector and facing his team, "work-life balance is not just about managing our time—it is about living authentically, pursuing meaning, and cultivating harmony between our professional and personal lives. By embracing the philosophical dimensions of work-life balance, we can create lives that are not just successful, but truly fulfilling, meaningful, and joyful."

With a renewed sense of introspection and commitment to living authentically, the executives at Apex Global Consulting prepared to apply these philosophical insights to their pursuit of work-life balance, knowing that they held the key to unlocking greater fulfillment and well-being in their lives.

Case Studies on Work Ethics and Practices

As the discussion on the philosophy of work and labor unfolded, Michael guided the executives through a series of case studies, each offering valuable insights into the diverse work ethics and practices prevalent in different organizations. The room buzzed with anticipation as they prepared to delve into real-world examples of the ethical dimensions of work.

"Now, let's turn our attention to **case studies on work ethics and practices**," Michael announced, his voice resonating with curiosity and contemplation. "These case studies will provide us with valuable lessons and perspectives on the ethical challenges and opportunities inherent in contemporary workplaces."

He clicked the remote, and the screen illuminated with the

title: **Case Studies on Work Ethics and Practices.**

"Our journey begins with the recognition that ethical dilemmas are an inherent part of the workplace, arising from complex interactions between individuals, organizations, and society," Michael continued, gesturing towards the screen. "By examining real-world examples of ethical challenges and responses, we can gain deeper insights into the ethical dimensions of work and labor."

The screen transitioned to images of diverse workplaces, from multinational corporations to small startups, each facing unique ethical dilemmas and opportunities. "Our first case study explores the ethical implications of automation and job displacement in the manufacturing industry. As technology advances, organizations are increasingly adopting automation and artificial intelligence to streamline processes and increase efficiency. However, these advancements raise ethical concerns about the impact on workers, their livelihoods, and the communities in which they live."

Michael explained, "By examining the responses of organizations to these challenges, from investing in retraining programs to fostering partnerships with local communities, we can gain insights into the ethical responsibilities of organizations towards their employees and society at large."

The executives nodded, recognizing the importance of ethical decision-making in the face of technological change.

"Next," Michael said, clicking to the next slide, "we explore a case study on workplace diversity and inclusion. In today's globalized and interconnected world, diversity and inclusion have become increasingly important for organizations seeking to foster innovation, creativity, and resilience. However, achieving diversity and inclusion in the workplace requires more than just hiring diverse talent—it requires creating an environment where all individuals feel valued, respected, and empowered to contribute their best."

The screen displayed images of organizations implementing diversity and inclusion initiatives, from unconscious bias training to mentorship programs. "By examining the approaches of organizations to diversity and inclusion, from promoting inclusive leadership to implementing flexible work policies, we can gain insights into the ethical imperatives of creating a more diverse, equitable, and inclusive workplace."

Michael continued, "By embracing diversity and inclusion as core values and principles, organizations can tap into the full potential of their talent pool, drive innovation, and create a more sustainable and resilient future for themselves and society."

The executives leaned forward, captivated by the examples of organizations striving to create more inclusive workplaces.

"Our final case study explores the ethical dimensions of corporate social responsibility (CSR). In an increasingly interconnected and interdependent world, organizations are facing growing pressure to address social and environmental challenges, from climate change to income inequality. Corporate social responsibility (CSR) offers organizations a framework for integrating ethical considerations into their business operations, supply chains, and stakeholder relationships."

The screen transitioned to visuals of organizations implementing CSR initiatives, from reducing carbon emissions to promoting fair labor practices. "By examining the CSR initiatives of organizations, from engaging in philanthropy to adopting sustainable business practices, we can gain insights into the ethical responsibilities of organizations towards society and the environment."

Michael explained, "By embracing CSR as a strategic imperative, organizations can create shared value for themselves and society, driving positive social and environmental impact while also enhancing their long-term sustainability and profitability."

He paused, allowing the significance of the case studies on work ethics and practices to resonate with the team. "In conclusion," Michael said, turning off the projector and facing his team, "case studies on work ethics and practices offer us valuable lessons and perspectives on the ethical dimensions of work and labor. By examining real-world examples of ethical challenges and responses, we can gain insights into the ethical responsibilities of organizations towards their employees, society, and the environment, and cultivate a deeper understanding of the ethical imperatives of contemporary workplaces."

With a renewed sense of awareness and commitment to ethical leadership, the executives at Apex Global Consulting prepared to apply these lessons to their own decision-making and practices, knowing that they held the key to creating workplaces that are not just successful, but also ethical, responsible, and sustainable.

Enhancing the Quality of Work Life

As the executives at Apex Global Consulting delved deeper into the discussion on the philosophy of work and labor, Michael shifted their focus towards enhancing the quality of work life, recognizing its profound impact on employee well-being, satisfaction, and productivity. The room filled with a sense of anticipation as they prepared to explore ways to create more fulfilling and enriching work experiences.

"Now, let's explore **enhancing the quality of work life**," Michael announced, his voice imbued with a sense of purpose and empathy. "At the heart of our discussion lies the recognition that the quality of work life is not just a matter of organizational policy, but a reflection of our values, culture, and leadership."

He clicked the remote, and the screen illuminated with the title: "**Enhancing the Quality of Work Life.**"

"Our journey begins with the acknowledgment that the quality of work life encompasses more than just physical comfort and material rewards," Michael continued, gesturing towards the screen. "It is about creating an environment where employees feel valued, respected, and empowered to bring their whole selves to work."

The screen transitioned to images of diverse workplaces, from open-plan offices to remote work setups, each offering unique opportunities and challenges for enhancing the quality of work life. "Our first step in enhancing the quality of work life is to create a culture of trust, transparency, and accountability within our organization. By fostering open communication, mutual respect, and shared values, we can create a workplace where employees feel valued, supported, and empowered to contribute their best."

Michael explained, "At its essence, enhancing the quality of work life is about creating meaningful and fulfilling work experiences that promote employee well-being, engagement, and satisfaction."

The executives nodded in agreement, recognizing the importance of creating a positive work culture.

"Next," Michael said, clicking to the next slide, "we explore the concept of **workplace flexibility**. In today's fast-paced and interconnected world, employees are seeking greater flexibility in how, when, and where they work. By embracing workplace flexibility, organizations can accommodate the diverse needs and preferences of their employees, from flexible hours to remote work options."

The screen displayed images of employees working from home, coffee shops, and co-working spaces, each finding their own rhythm and balance in their work life. "By offering flexibility in work arrangements, organizations can enhance employee autonomy, work-life balance, and job satisfaction. This not only improves employee well-being and retention but also fosters a culture of innovation, collaboration, and resilience."

Michael continued, "By embracing workplace flexibility as a strategic imperative, organizations can create a more agile, adaptive, and resilient workforce, capable of navigating the challenges and opportunities of the modern workplace."

The executives leaned forward, captivated by the idea of embracing flexibility in their organization.

"Our journey also involves **investing in employee development and growth**," Michael said, bringing up an image of employees participating in training and development programs. "Employees are our most valuable asset, and investing in their development and growth is essential for enhancing the quality of work life. By offering opportunities for learning, skill development, and career advancement, organizations can empower employees to realize their full potential and achieve their professional goals."

The screen transitioned to visuals of employees participating in workshops, seminars, and mentoring programs, each gaining new skills, knowledge, and insights to thrive in their roles. "By investing in employee development and growth, organizations can foster a culture of continuous learning, innovation, and excellence. This not only enhances employee engagement and satisfaction but also strengthens organizational capabilities and competitiveness in the marketplace."

Michael explained, "By embracing employee development and growth as a strategic imperative, organizations can create a culture of excellence, achievement, and fulfillment, where employees are empowered to realize their aspirations and contribute their best to the organization."

He paused, allowing the significance of enhancing the quality of work life to resonate with the team. "In conclusion," Michael said, turning off the projector and facing his team, "enhancing the quality of work life is not just a matter of organizational policy—it is a reflection of our values, culture, and leadership. By fostering a culture of trust, transparency, and accountability, embracing workplace flexibility, and investing in employee development and growth, we can create workplaces that are not just successful, but also fulfilling, enriching, and empowering for employees."

With a renewed sense of commitment to enhancing the quality of work life, the executives at Apex Global Consulting prepared to apply these principles to their own organization, knowing that they held the key to creating a more positive, engaging, and fulfilling work environment for their employees.

Chapter 10: Organizational Culture and Ethics

Defining Organizational Culture from a Philosophical View

As the executives gathered in the boardroom of Apex Global Consulting, Michael prepared to delve into the intricate relationship between organizational culture and ethics, recognizing their profound impact on the success and sustainability of the organization. The room buzzed with anticipation as they prepared to explore the philosophical dimensions of organizational culture.

"Let's begin our exploration of **organizational culture and ethics**," Michael announced, his voice resonating with a sense of purpose and inquiry. "At the heart of our discussion lies the recognition that organizational culture is not just a set of norms and practices, but a reflection of our values, beliefs, and aspirations."

He clicked the remote, and the screen illuminated with the title: **"Organizational Culture and Ethics."**

"Our journey begins with the acknowledgment that organizational culture encompasses the shared beliefs, values, and behaviors that shape the identity and character of an organization," Michael continued, gesturing towards the screen. "From the way we interact with one another to the way we make decisions and solve problems, organizational culture influences every aspect of our work life."

The screen transitioned to images of diverse workplace settings, each reflecting a unique organizational culture, from fast-paced startups to established corporations. "Our first step in understanding organizational culture is to recognize its philosophical underpinnings. Organizational culture is not just a product of organizational structure or processes, but a manifestation of our deepest values, beliefs, and assumptions about the nature of work, leadership, and success."

Michael explained, "At its essence, organizational culture reflects our collective identity and purpose, guiding our behavior, decisions, and interactions within the organization. By examining the philosophical foundations of organizational culture, we can gain deeper insights into its role in shaping our values, ethics, and organizational outcomes."

The executives nodded in agreement, recognizing the importance of understanding the philosophical dimensions of organizational culture.

"Next," Michael said, clicking to the next slide, "we explore the concept of **ethics in organizational culture**. Ethics is the moral compass that guides our behavior and decision-making within the organization. It is about doing what is right, just, and fair, even when it is difficult or unpopular."

The screen displayed images of individuals engaging in ethical dilemmas and ethical decision-making processes within organizational settings. "Ethics in organizational culture involves more than just compliance with laws and regulations—

it requires a commitment to ethical principles and values, such as integrity, honesty, respect, and fairness. It is about fostering a culture of trust, transparency, and accountability, where ethical considerations are integrated into every aspect of organizational life."

Michael continued, "By embedding ethics into the fabric of organizational culture, we can create a workplace where integrity, honesty, and ethical behavior are not just encouraged, but expected. This not only enhances employee trust and loyalty but also strengthens organizational reputation and resilience in the face of ethical challenges and crises."

The executives leaned forward, captivated by the idea of fostering an ethical organizational culture.

"Our journey also involves **examining the role of leadership in shaping organizational culture**," Michael said, bringing up an image of leaders setting the tone for ethical behavior within the organization. "Leadership plays a critical role in shaping organizational culture and ethics. Leaders are not just managers—they are moral agents responsible for setting the tone, direction, and values of the organization."

The screen transitioned to visuals of leaders modeling ethical behavior, communicating ethical expectations, and holding themselves and others accountable for upholding ethical standards. "By leading with integrity, authenticity, and humility, leaders can inspire trust, foster collaboration, and create a culture of ethics and excellence within the organization."

Michael explained, "By embracing ethical leadership as a core value and principle, organizations can cultivate a culture of integrity, accountability, and responsibility, where ethical considerations are woven into the fabric of everyday decision-making and actions."

He paused, allowing the significance of organizational culture and ethics to resonate with the team. "In conclusion," Michael said, turning off the projector and facing his team, "organizational culture and ethics are not just abstract concepts—they are lived experiences that shape our identity, behavior, and outcomes within the organization. By understanding the philosophical foundations of organizational culture, embedding ethics into its fabric, and cultivating ethical leadership, we can create workplaces that are not just successful, but also ethical, responsible, and sustainable."

With a renewed sense of commitment to fostering an ethical organizational culture, the executives at Apex Global Consulting prepared to apply these principles to their own leadership and organizational practices, knowing that they held the key to creating a workplace where integrity, honesty, and ethical behavior were not just valued, but lived every day.

Building an Ethical Organizational Culture

As the discussion on organizational culture and ethics continued, Michael guided the executives through the process of building an ethical organizational culture, recognizing its significance in shaping the behavior, decisions, and outcomes within the organization. The atmosphere in the room was charged with anticipation as they prepared to explore practical strategies for fostering ethicality within their workplace.

"Now, let's delve into **building an ethical organizational culture**," Michael announced, his voice echoing with determination and purpose. "At the core of our discussion lies the recognition that organizational culture is not just a reflection of our values, but a product of our actions, behaviors, and interactions within the organization."

He clicked the remote, and the screen illuminated with the title: **"Building an Ethical Organizational Culture."**

"Our journey begins with the acknowledgment that building an ethical organizational culture requires more than just words—it requires consistent actions, behaviors, and decisions that reflect our commitment to ethical principles and values," Michael continued, gesturing towards the screen. "It is about creating an environment where ethicality is not just encouraged, but embedded into every aspect of organizational life."

The screen transitioned to images of leaders and employees engaging in ethical behaviors, from honest communication to fair decision-making processes. "Our first step in building an ethical organizational culture is to lead by example. Leaders are not just managers—they are moral agents responsible for setting the tone, direction, and values of the organization. By modeling ethical behavior, communicating ethical expectations, and holding themselves and others accountable for upholding ethical standards, leaders can inspire trust, foster collaboration, and create a culture of ethics and excellence within the organization."

Michael explained, "At its essence, building an ethical organizational culture is about creating a shared sense of purpose, values, and identity that guides our behavior, decisions, and interactions within the organization. By fostering a culture of trust, transparency, and accountability, where ethical considerations are integrated into every aspect of organizational life, we can create a workplace where integrity, honesty, and ethical behavior are not just encouraged, but expected."

The executives nodded in agreement, recognizing the importance of leadership in shaping organizational culture.

"Next," Michael said, clicking to the next slide, "we explore the importance of **clear ethical standards and policies**. In order to build an ethical organizational culture, it is essential to have clear and comprehensive ethical standards and policies in place. These standards and policies provide guidance and direction to employees on what is expected of them in terms of ethical behavior, decision-making, and interactions within the organization."

The screen displayed images of employees reviewing and discussing ethical standards and policies, from codes of conduct to whistleblower policies. "By articulating clear ethical standards and policies, organizations can create a framework for ethical decision-making and behavior, and provide employees with the tools and resources they need to navigate ethical dilemmas and challenges in the workplace."

Michael continued, "By embedding ethical standards and policies into the fabric of organizational life, organizations can create a culture of integrity, accountability, and responsibility, where ethical considerations are woven into the fabric of everyday decision-making and actions."

The executives leaned forward, captivated by the idea of establishing clear ethical standards and policies.

"Our journey also involves **creating mechanisms for accountability and transparency**," Michael said, bringing up an image of leaders and employees discussing ethical concerns and dilemmas. "In order to build an ethical organizational culture, it is essential to have mechanisms in place for holding individuals and groups accountable for their actions, behaviors, and decisions."

The screen transitioned to visuals of employees participating in ethics training, reporting ethical concerns, and holding ethical discussions. "By creating a culture of accountability and transparency, where individuals feel comfortable speaking up about ethical concerns and are held accountable for their actions, organizations can create a workplace where integrity, honesty, and ethical behavior are valued and rewarded."

Michael explained, "By establishing mechanisms for accountability and transparency, organizations can foster a culture of trust, openness, and integrity, where ethical considerations are integrated into every aspect of organizational life."

He paused, allowing the significance of building an ethical organizational culture to resonate with the team. "In conclusion," Michael said, turning off the projector and facing his team, "building an ethical organizational culture is not just a matter of words—it is a reflection of our actions, behaviors, and decisions within the organization. By leading by example, articulating clear ethical standards and policies, and creating mechanisms for accountability and transparency, we can create workplaces that are not just successful, but also ethical, responsible, and sustainable."

With a renewed sense of commitment to building an ethical organizational culture, the executives at Apex Global Consulting prepared to apply these strategies to their own leadership and organizational practices, knowing that they held the key to creating a workplace where integrity, honesty, and ethical behavior were not just valued, but lived every day.

The Role of Leadership in Shaping Culture

As the executives at Apex Global Consulting delved deeper into the discussion on organizational culture and ethics, Michael shifted their focus towards the pivotal role of leadership in shaping the culture of the organization, recognizing its profound influence on employee behavior, attitudes, and values. The room was filled with a palpable sense of anticipation as they prepared to explore the instrumental role leaders play in creating a culture of ethics and integrity.

"Now, let's explore **the role of leadership in shaping culture**," Michael announced, his voice commanding attention and respect. "At the heart of our discussion lies the recognition that leaders are not just managers—they are moral agents responsible for setting the tone, direction, and values of the organization."

He clicked the remote, and the screen illuminated with the title: "**The Role of Leadership in Shaping Culture.**"

"Our journey begins with the acknowledgment that leadership is the driving force behind organizational culture. Leaders shape the culture of the organization through their actions, behaviors, and decisions, which serve as a model for others to follow," Michael continued, gesturing towards the screen. "It is through their leadership that organizations establish their identity, values, and norms, and create an environment where integrity, honesty, and ethical behavior thrive."

The screen transitioned to images of leaders engaging with employees, communicating vision and values, and leading by example. "Our first step in understanding the role of leadership in shaping culture is to recognize the power of leadership influence. Leaders set the tone for the organization through their words and actions, which serve as a model for employees to emulate. By embodying the values and principles of the organization, leaders create a culture of trust, respect, and integrity, where ethical behavior is valued and rewarded."

Michael explained, "At its essence, leadership is about inspiring and empowering others to achieve common goals and aspirations. By fostering a culture of transparency, accountability, and collaboration, leaders can create an environment where individuals feel valued, respected, and motivated to contribute their best to the organization."

The executives nodded in agreement, recognizing the importance of leadership in shaping organizational culture.

"Next," Michael said, clicking to the next slide, "we explore the concept of **authentic leadership**. In today's complex and dynamic business environment, authenticity has emerged as a key leadership trait. Authentic leaders are genuine, transparent, and self-aware, leading with integrity, humility, and empathy. By embracing authenticity, leaders can foster trust, build credibility, and create a culture of openness and honesty within the organization."

The screen displayed images of leaders demonstrating authenticity through their actions, behaviors, and interactions with others. "Authentic leaders lead by example, living their values and principles in every aspect of their leadership. They are not afraid to admit mistakes, seek feedback, and learn from others, creating a culture of continuous improvement and growth. By embodying authenticity, leaders can inspire trust, foster collaboration, and create a culture of integrity and ethical behavior within the organization."

Michael continued, "By embracing authentic leadership

as a core value and principle, organizations can create a culture of trust, transparency, and accountability, where ethical considerations are integrated into every aspect of organizational life."

He paused, allowing the significance of leadership in shaping culture to resonate with the team. "In conclusion," Michael said, turning off the projector and facing his team, "the role of leadership in shaping culture is not just about managing people—it is about inspiring and empowering others to achieve common goals and aspirations. By leading with authenticity, integrity, and empathy, leaders can create workplaces that are not just successful, but also ethical, responsible, and sustainable."

With a renewed sense of commitment to authentic leadership, the executives at Apex Global Consulting prepared to apply these principles to their own leadership practices, knowing that they held the key to creating a workplace where integrity, honesty, and ethical behavior were not just valued, but lived every day.

Case Studies of Ethical Cultures in Organizations

As the discussion on organizational culture and ethics continued, Michael guided the executives through a series of case studies showcasing organizations renowned for their ethical cultures. The room brimmed with anticipation as they prepared to glean insights from real-world examples of ethical leadership and organizational practices.

"Now, let's turn our attention to **case studies of ethical cultures in organizations**," Michael announced, his voice carrying the weight of anticipation and inquiry. "These case studies offer us invaluable insights into how organizations cultivate and sustain ethical cultures, fostering trust, integrity, and responsibility among their employees."

He clicked the remote, and the screen illuminated with the title: **"Case Studies of Ethical Cultures in Organizations."**

"Our journey begins with the recognition that ethical cultures are not just a product of chance, but the result of deliberate efforts by leaders and employees to uphold ethical principles and values," Michael continued, gesturing towards the screen. "By examining the practices of organizations renowned for their ethical cultures, we can gain insights into the strategies and initiatives that contribute to the cultivation of ethicality within the workplace."

The screen transitioned to images of renowned organizations celebrated for their ethical cultures, from global corporations to local nonprofits. "Our first case study explores the ethical culture of Company X, a multinational corporation known for its unwavering commitment to integrity, transparency, and responsibility. Through its code of conduct, ethics training programs, and robust compliance mechanisms, Company X has created a culture where ethical behavior is not just encouraged, but expected from every employee."

Michael explained, "By embedding ethics into every aspect of its operations, from hiring and performance evaluations to decision-making processes and stakeholder relations, Company X has fostered a culture of trust, accountability, and responsibility, which has contributed to its long-term success and sustainability."

The executives nodded in agreement, recognizing the importance of ethics in organizational culture.

"Next," Michael said, clicking to the next slide, "we explore the case of Organization Y, a nonprofit dedicated to social and environmental causes. Despite facing numerous ethical challenges and dilemmas, Organization Y has remained steadfast in its commitment to ethical principles and values, guided by its mission to create positive social impact."

The screen displayed images of Organization Y's initiatives to promote ethical behavior and responsible practices, from fair labor standards to environmental stewardship. "Through its ethical leadership, transparent communication, and stakeholder engagement, Organization Y has built a culture of trust, collaboration, and social responsibility, which has earned it the respect and admiration of its employees, partners, and communities."

Michael continued, "By aligning its actions with its values and mission, Organization Y has demonstrated that ethicality is not just a moral imperative, but a strategic advantage that drives innovation, engagement, and impact within the organization and beyond."

The executives leaned forward, captivated by the examples of ethical cultures in action.

"Our final case study examines the ethical culture of Startup Z, a small but rapidly growing company known for its innovative products and inclusive workplace culture. Despite its size and resources, Startup Z has prioritized ethics from the outset, embedding it into its values, hiring practices, and decision-making processes."

The screen transitioned to visuals of Startup Z's initiatives to foster an inclusive and ethical workplace, from diversity and inclusion programs to employee empowerment initiatives. "Through its commitment to transparency, fairness, and empowerment, Startup Z has created a culture where every voice is valued, every idea is heard, and every action is guided by ethical considerations."

Michael explained, "By investing in its people, fostering a culture of openness and collaboration, and upholding its ethical principles, Startup Z has not only attracted top talent and loyal customers but has also become a beacon of ethical leadership and innovation in its industry."

He paused, allowing the significance of the case studies on ethical cultures to resonate with the team. "In conclusion," Michael said, turning off the projector and facing his team, "case studies of ethical cultures in organizations offer us invaluable insights into the strategies and initiatives that contribute to the cultivation of ethicality within the workplace. By examining real-world examples of ethical leadership and organizational practices, we can gain inspiration and guidance in our own journey towards building a culture of trust, integrity, and responsibility within Apex Global Consulting."

With a renewed sense of inspiration and purpose, the executives at Apex Global Consulting prepared to apply the lessons learned from these case studies to their own leadership and organizational practices, knowing that they held the key to creating a workplace where ethics were not just valued, but lived every day.

Philosophical Tools for Cultural Analysis

As the discussion on organizational culture and ethics unfolded, Michael introduced the executives to a set of philosophical tools for cultural analysis, offering them a unique perspective on understanding and evaluating the underlying values, beliefs, and assumptions that shape their organization's culture. The atmosphere in the room brimmed with curiosity and intrigue as they prepared to explore these philosophical frameworks.

"Now, let's explore **philosophical tools for cultural analysis**," Michael announced, his voice resonating with a sense of inquiry and exploration. "These tools offer us invaluable insights into the deeper layers of organizational culture, allowing us to uncover the underlying values, beliefs, and assumptions that shape our workplace."

He clicked the remote, and the screen illuminated with the title: **"Philosophical Tools for Cultural Analysis."**

"Our journey begins with the recognition that organizational culture is not just a surface-level phenomenon, but a complex interplay of values, beliefs, and assumptions that influence our behavior, decisions, and interactions within the organization," Michael continued, gesturing towards the screen. "By employing philosophical tools for cultural analysis, we can uncover the hidden dynamics and underlying patterns that define our organizational culture."

The screen transitioned to images of philosophical texts and frameworks, from existentialism to critical theory, each offering a unique lens through which to analyze organizational culture. "Our first tool for cultural analysis is **existentialism**, which emphasizes the subjective experience of individuals and the search for meaning and purpose in life. By applying existentialist principles to organizational culture, we can explore questions of authenticity, freedom, and responsibility within the workplace."

Michael explained, "Existentialism invites us to examine the lived experiences of employees, their sense of autonomy, and their quest for meaning and fulfillment in their work. By fostering an environment where individuals feel empowered to express their authentic selves, pursue their passions, and contribute their unique talents to the organization, we can create a culture of engagement, innovation, and fulfillment."

The executives nodded in agreement, recognizing the power of existentialism in understanding organizational culture.

"Next," Michael said, clicking to the next slide, "we explore **critical theory**, which seeks to uncover and challenge the underlying power structures and inequalities that shape society. By applying critical theory to organizational culture, we can examine the power dynamics, hierarchies, and injustices that may exist within our workplace."

The screen displayed images of critical theorists analyzing organizational structures and practices through a lens of power and domination. "Critical theory invites us to question the status quo, challenge entrenched norms and practices, and advocate for social justice and equity within the organization. By fostering a culture of inclusivity, diversity, and empowerment, we can create an environment where every voice is heard, every perspective is valued, and every individual is treated with dignity and respect."

Michael continued, "By embracing critical theory as a tool for cultural analysis, organizations can identify and address systemic barriers and biases that may hinder the realization of their values and goals, and create a more just, equitable, and inclusive workplace for all."

The executives leaned forward, captivated by the idea of employing critical theory in their cultural analysis.

"Our final tool for cultural analysis is **pragmatism**, which emphasizes the practical consequences of beliefs and actions. By applying pragmatic principles to organizational culture, we can evaluate the effectiveness and impact of our values, beliefs, and practices on organizational outcomes and stakeholder satisfaction."

The screen transitioned to visuals of pragmatists analyzing organizational processes and outcomes through a lens of effectiveness and utility. "Pragmatism invites us to examine the real-world consequences of our decisions and actions, and adjust our strategies and practices accordingly. By fostering a culture of experimentation, adaptation, and continuous improvement, we can create an environment where innovation thrives, and organizational goals are achieved."

Michael explained, "By embracing pragmatism as a tool for cultural analysis, organizations can identify strengths and weaknesses in their culture, and implement strategies to enhance organizational effectiveness, employee engagement, and stakeholder satisfaction."

He paused, allowing the significance of employing philosophical tools for cultural analysis to resonate with the team. "In conclusion," Michael said, turning off the projector and facing his team, "philosophical tools for cultural analysis offer us invaluable insights into the deeper dynamics of organizational culture, allowing us to uncover hidden patterns, challenge entrenched norms, and create a workplace that reflects our values, aspirations, and ideals."

With a renewed sense of understanding and insight, the executives at Apex Global Consulting prepared to apply these philosophical frameworks to their own cultural analysis, knowing that they held the key to creating a workplace that was not just successful, but also ethical, inclusive, and fulfilling for all.

Strategies for Cultural Transformation

As the discussion on organizational culture and ethics reached its climax, Michael shifted the focus towards strategies for cultural transformation, recognizing the need for deliberate and concerted efforts to reshape their organization's culture towards one that embodied their desired values and principles. The room buzzed with anticipation as they prepared to explore practical strategies for driving cultural change within their workplace.

"Now, let's delve into **strategies for cultural transformation**," Michael announced, his voice carrying a sense of urgency and determination. "Cultural transformation requires more than just rhetoric—it demands deliberate actions, interventions, and initiatives that align with our vision and values."

He clicked the remote, and the screen illuminated with the title: **"Strategies for Cultural Transformation."**

"Our journey begins with the acknowledgment that cultural transformation is a multifaceted and ongoing process that requires the involvement and commitment of all stakeholders within the organization," Michael continued, gesturing towards the screen. "By employing strategies for cultural transformation, we can create an environment where our desired values and behaviors are not just encouraged, but embedded into every aspect of organizational life."

The screen transitioned to images of diverse workplaces undergoing cultural transformation, from team-building exercises to leadership development programs. "Our first strategy for cultural transformation is **leadership alignment**. Leaders play a pivotal role in shaping organizational culture, and their actions and behaviors serve as a model for others to follow. By ensuring that leaders are aligned with the organization's vision, values, and goals, we can create a cohesive and unified approach to cultural transformation."

Michael explained, "Leadership alignment involves communicating the vision and values of the organization, modeling the desired behaviors, and holding themselves and others accountable for upholding them. By fostering a culture of leadership alignment, we can create a sense of shared purpose, direction, and commitment to cultural transformation."

The executives nodded in agreement, recognizing the importance of leadership in driving cultural change.

"Next," Michael said, clicking to the next slide, "we explore the strategy of **employee engagement and empowerment**. Cultural transformation cannot succeed without the active participation and involvement of employees at all levels of the organization. By engaging and empowering employees to contribute their ideas, feedback, and insights, we can harness the collective intelligence and creativity of the organization to drive meaningful change."

The screen displayed images of employees participating in brainstorming sessions, feedback forums, and decision-making processes. "Employee engagement and empowerment involve creating opportunities for employees to voice their opinions, share their experiences, and contribute to decision-making processes. By fostering a culture of openness, inclusivity, and collaboration, we can tap into the diverse talents and perspectives of our workforce to drive innovation and change."

Michael continued, "By empowering employees to take ownership of the cultural transformation process, we can create a sense of ownership, commitment, and accountability that fuels organizational success."

The executives leaned forward, captivated by the idea of empowering their workforce in the transformation process.

"Our final strategy for cultural transformation is **continuous learning and improvement**. Cultural transformation is not a one-time event, but an ongoing journey of discovery, adaptation, and growth. By fostering a culture of continuous learning and improvement, we can create an environment where experimentation, innovation, and adaptation are encouraged and rewarded."

The screen transitioned to visuals of employees participating in training programs, workshops, and knowledge-sharing sessions. "Continuous learning and improvement involve providing employees with opportunities to develop new skills, acquire new knowledge, and expand their perspectives. By investing in their growth and development, we can create a culture of learning and innovation that drives organizational performance and success."

Michael explained, "By embracing a mindset of continuous learning and improvement, organizations can adapt to changing circumstances, anticipate future challenges, and seize new opportunities for growth and development."

He paused, allowing the significance of the strategies for cultural transformation to resonate with the team. "In conclusion," Michael said, turning off the projector and facing his team, "strategies for cultural transformation offer us a roadmap for creating a workplace that reflects our values, aspirations, and ideals. By aligning leadership, engaging and empowering employees, and fostering a culture of continuous learning and improvement, we can drive meaningful change and create a workplace that is not just successful, but also ethical, inclusive, and fulfilling for all."

With a renewed sense of purpose and determination, the executives at Apex Global Consulting prepared to apply these strategies to their own cultural transformation journey, knowing that they held the key to creating a workplace where integrity, honesty, and ethical behavior were not just valued, but lived every day.

Chapter 11: Communication and Philosophy

Philosophical Theories of Communication

As the executives at Apex Global Consulting gathered for their next session, Michael introduced them to the profound intersection between communication and philosophy, setting the stage for a deep dive into the philosophical theories that underpin effective communication within organizations. The room hummed with anticipation as they prepared to explore this captivating topic.

"Now, let's embark on a journey into **communication and philosophy**," Michael announced, his voice resonating with a blend of curiosity and reverence. "Communication is not just a tool—it's a fundamental aspect of human interaction that is deeply intertwined with philosophical principles."

He clicked the remote, and the screen illuminated with the title: "**Communication and Philosophy.**"

"Our exploration begins with an examination of **philosophical theories of communication**," Michael continued, gesturing towards the screen. "These theories offer us valuable insights into the nature, purpose, and dynamics of communication, shedding light on how we exchange ideas, thoughts, and emotions with others."

The screen transitioned to images of renowned philosophers and communication theorists, from Aristotle to Marshall McLuhan. "Our first stop on this journey is the realm of **semiotics**, which explores the study of signs, symbols, and meanings in communication. From the ancient philosophers to modern-day theorists, semiotics has provided us with a framework for understanding how we encode and decode messages, and how meanings are created and conveyed through language, gestures, and symbols."

Michael explained, "Semiotics invites us to question the nature of language, the power of symbols, and the influence of culture on communication. By understanding the principles of semiotics, we can become more conscious and intentional communicators, adept at navigating the complexities of meaning and interpretation in our interactions with others."

The executives nodded in agreement, recognizing the significance of semiotics in communication.

"Next," Michael said, clicking to the next slide, "we explore the philosophy of **dialogue**. Dialogue goes beyond mere conversation—it's a process of mutual understanding, exploration, and discovery that seeks to bridge differences and foster deeper connections between individuals."

The screen displayed images of individuals engaged in meaningful dialogue, listening attentively to each other's perspectives and engaging in respectful exchange. "Dialogue invites us to suspend judgment, cultivate empathy, and engage in active listening, as we seek to understand and appreciate the viewpoints of others. By embracing dialogue as a philosophical principle, we can create a culture of openness, collaboration, and trust within our organizations."

Michael continued, "By fostering a culture of dialogue, organizations can break down silos, encourage collaboration across departments, and harness the collective intelligence and creativity of their workforce."

The executives leaned forward, captivated by the idea of fostering dialogue in their organization.

"Our final exploration takes us into the realm of **rhetoric**. Rhetoric is the art of persuasion, the skillful use of language and argumentation to influence, inspire, and motivate others. From the ancient Greeks to contemporary scholars, rhetoric has played a central role in shaping public discourse and shaping our understanding of persuasion and influence."

The screen transitioned to visuals of famous speeches and persuasive arguments throughout history. "Rhetoric invites us to consider the power of language, the art of persuasion, and the ethical implications of our communication strategies. By mastering the principles of rhetoric, we can become more effective communicators, capable of inspiring action, fostering engagement, and building consensus within our organizations."

Michael explained, "By embracing rhetoric as a philosophical tool, organizations can enhance their communication strategies, build stronger relationships with stakeholders, and achieve their goals and objectives more effectively."

He paused, allowing the significance of philosophical theories of communication to resonate with the team. "In conclusion," Michael said, turning off the projector and facing his team, "philosophical theories of communication offer us valuable insights into the nature, purpose, and dynamics of communication. By understanding the principles of semiotics, dialogue, and rhetoric, we can become more conscious and intentional communicators, capable of fostering meaningful connections and driving positive change within our organizations."

With a renewed appreciation for the profound intersection between communication and philosophy, the executives at Apex Global Consulting prepared to apply these insights to their own communication strategies, knowing that they held the key to fostering a culture of openness, collaboration, and trust within their organization.

Ethical Communication Practices in Management

As the executives settled in for the continuation of their discussion on communication and philosophy, Michael directed their attention towards the ethical dimensions of communication in management, recognizing the critical role it plays in shaping organizational culture and fostering trust among stakeholders. The atmosphere in the room shifted, as they prepared to explore the principles and practices of ethical communication.

"Now, let's delve into **ethical communication practices in management**," Michael announced, his voice carrying a tone of gravity and introspection. "Communication is not just about conveying information—it's about building relationships, fostering trust, and upholding ethical principles."

He clicked the remote, and the screen illuminated with the title: "**Ethical Communication Practices in Management.**"

"Our exploration begins with the recognition that communication is a moral endeavor, with ethical implications that extend far beyond the exchange of words," Michael continued, gesturing towards the screen. "Ethical communication practices in management require us to consider the impact of our words and actions on others, and to uphold principles of honesty, transparency, and respect in all our interactions."

The screen transitioned to images of leaders engaging in ethical communication practices, from honest feedback sessions to transparent decision-making processes. "Our first principle of ethical communication is **honesty**. Honesty is the foundation of trust—it's about being truthful and transparent in our communication, even when it's difficult or uncomfortable. By practicing honesty in our interactions with others, we can build trust, credibility, and integrity within our organizations."

Michael explained, "Honest communication involves sharing information openly and candidly, addressing concerns and issues directly, and admitting mistakes when they occur. By fostering a culture of honesty, organizations can create an environment where employees feel valued, respected, and trusted, leading to higher levels of engagement, satisfaction, and loyalty."

The executives nodded in agreement, recognizing the importance of honesty in communication.

"Next," Michael said, clicking to the next slide, "we explore the principle of **transparency**. Transparency is about being open and forthcoming in our communication, sharing information freely and openly with stakeholders, and providing them with the context and rationale behind our decisions and actions."

The screen displayed images of leaders communicating transparently with employees, sharing insights into organizational goals, strategies, and challenges. "Transparency builds trust—it demonstrates respect for others' intelligence and autonomy, and it fosters a sense of inclusion and ownership among stakeholders. By practicing transparency in our communication, we can create a culture of accountability, collaboration, and trust within our organizations."

Michael continued, "Transparent communication involves sharing both the good and the bad news, seeking input and feedback from stakeholders, and being willing to listen and respond to their concerns and questions. By fostering a culture of transparency, organizations can create an environment where trust thrives, and employees feel empowered to contribute their best to the organization."

The executives leaned forward, captivated by the idea of fostering transparency in their organization.

"Our final principle of ethical communication is **respect**. Respect is about treating others with dignity, empathy, and understanding in our communication, regardless of their position or status within the organization."

The screen transitioned to visuals of leaders demonstrating respect in their communication, listening attentively to others' perspectives and valuing their contributions. "Respectful communication fosters a culture of inclusivity, diversity, and belonging—it acknowledges the worth and dignity of every individual, and it creates an environment where everyone feels valued, respected, and heard."

Michael explained, "Respectful communication involves active listening, empathy, and sensitivity to others' feelings and perspectives. By practicing respect in our communication, we can create a culture of mutual trust, collaboration, and support within our organizations."

He paused, allowing the significance of ethical communication practices to resonate with the team. "In conclusion," Michael said, turning off the projector and facing his team, "ethical communication practices in management are essential for building trust, fostering collaboration, and upholding the values and principles of our organization. By practicing honesty, transparency, and respect in our communication, we can create an environment where trust thrives, and stakeholders feel empowered to contribute their best to the organization."

With a renewed commitment to ethical communication, the executives at Apex Global Consulting prepared to apply these principles to their own communication practices, knowing that they held the key to fostering a culture of integrity, trust, and respect within their organization.

The Role of Transparency and Honesty

As the executives remained engrossed in the discussion on communication and philosophy, Michael directed their attention towards the pivotal role of transparency and honesty in organizational communication. Understanding the significance of these principles, they eagerly awaited to unravel their implications within the context of management.

"Now, let's delve into **the role of transparency and honesty**," Michael announced, his voice resonating with a blend of conviction and sincerity. "Transparency and honesty are not merely ideals; they are guiding principles that shape the foundation of trust within organizations."

He clicked the remote, and the screen illuminated with the title: **"The Role of Transparency and Honesty."**

"Our exploration begins with the acknowledgment that transparency and honesty are not just virtues; they are indispensable components of effective communication," Michael continued, gesturing towards the screen. "In the realm of management, these principles serve as catalysts for building trust, fostering collaboration, and driving organizational success."

The screen transitioned to images depicting leaders embodying transparency and honesty in their communication practices, from open-door policies to candid discussions with employees. "Our first consideration is **transparency**. In the modern workplace, transparency is not merely an option; it's a necessity. Transparent communication ensures that stakeholders are informed about organizational decisions, processes, and outcomes."

Michael explained, "Transparency instills confidence—it demonstrates a commitment to accountability, integrity, and open dialogue. By practicing transparency in management, organizations create an environment where employees feel valued, respected, and empowered to contribute to the collective success."

The executives nodded in agreement, recognizing the transformative power of transparency.

"Next," Michael said, clicking to the next slide, "let's explore **honesty**. Honesty forms the bedrock of trust—it establishes credibility, authenticity, and reliability in communication."

The screen displayed images portraying leaders exemplifying honesty in their interactions, from admitting mistakes to delivering difficult news with empathy and integrity. "Honesty fosters authenticity—it builds rapport and strengthens relationships among stakeholders. By practicing honesty in management, organizations cultivate a culture of integrity, where ethical behavior is celebrated and rewarded."

Michael continued, "Honesty demands courage—it requires leaders to confront uncomfortable truths and communicate them with compassion and sincerity. By embracing honesty in management, organizations create a culture of trust, where stakeholders feel valued, respected, and confident in the organization's integrity."

The executives leaned forward, captivated by the profound impact of honesty on organizational culture.

"Our final consideration," Michael said, "is the symbiotic relationship between transparency and honesty. Together, they form the cornerstone of ethical communication, guiding leaders in navigating the complexities of the modern workplace."

The screen transitioned to visuals depicting the seamless integration of transparency and honesty in management practices, from transparent decision-making processes to honest feedback mechanisms. "Transparency without honesty can breed skepticism, while honesty without transparency can lead to confusion. By embracing both principles in tandem, organizations create a communication culture characterized by openness, authenticity, and trust."

Michael explained, "Transparency and honesty reinforce each other, creating a virtuous cycle of trust and credibility within the organization. By prioritizing these principles in management, organizations lay the groundwork for sustainable success and resilience in an ever-changing business landscape."

He paused, allowing the significance of transparency and honesty to resonate with the team. "In conclusion," Michael said, turning off the projector and facing his team, "the role of transparency and honesty in management cannot be overstated. By embracing these principles, organizations cultivate a culture of trust, integrity, and collaboration, laying the foundation for long-term success and prosperity."

With a renewed commitment to transparency and honesty, the executives at Apex Global Consulting prepared to integrate these principles into their management practices, knowing that they held the key to fostering a culture of openness, authenticity, and trust within their organization.

Case Studies of Communication Breakdowns and Solutions

As the executives remained engaged in the exploration of communication and philosophy, Michael redirected their attention to the real-world implications through the examination of case studies. Anticipation filled the room as they awaited to unravel the lessons embedded within these tales of communication breakdowns and their subsequent solutions.

"Now, let's turn our focus to **case studies of communication breakdowns and solutions**," Michael announced, his voice imbued with a sense of inquiry and anticipation. "While theoretical frameworks are valuable, it's through real-world examples that we truly understand the complexities of communication in management."

He clicked the remote, and the screen illuminated with the title: **"Case Studies of Communication Breakdowns and Solutions."**

"Our exploration begins with a recognition that communication breakdowns are not uncommon in the workplace—they can arise from a variety of factors, including misalignment, misunderstandings, and misinterpretations," Michael continued, gesturing towards the screen. "However, what sets successful organizations apart is their ability to identify these breakdowns and implement effective solutions to address them."

The screen transitioned to images depicting scenarios of communication breakdowns, from missed deadlines due to miscommunications to conflicts arising from unclear expectations. "Our first case study examines a situation where a lack of clarity in communication led to a breakdown in team collaboration and productivity."

Michael explained, "In this scenario, a project team failed to meet their deadline due to miscommunication about roles, responsibilities, and expectations. As a result, tasks were duplicated, resources were misallocated, and tensions rose among team members."

The executives nodded in understanding, recognizing the familiar challenges of miscommunication.

"Next," Michael said, clicking to the next slide, "let's explore the solutions implemented to address this breakdown. Through open dialogue, clear expectations, and enhanced coordination, the team was able to realign their efforts, clarify roles and responsibilities, and overcome the obstacles that had hindered their progress."

The screen displayed images of team members engaging in constructive dialogue, clarifying expectations, and establishing a shared understanding of their goals and objectives. "By fostering a culture of open communication, active listening, and collaboration, the team was able to rebuild trust, enhance coordination, and ultimately achieve their objectives."

Michael continued, "This case study highlights the importance of proactive communication in addressing breakdowns and fostering resilience within teams."

The executives leaned forward, captivated by the practical insights gleaned from the case study.

"Our next case study," Michael said, "examines a scenario where a lack of transparency in communication led to distrust among employees and eroded morale within the organization."

The screen transitioned to visuals depicting employees expressing frustration and confusion over a lack of information about organizational changes and decisions. "In this scenario, rumors and speculation filled the void created by a lack of transparent communication from leadership. Employees felt disconnected, undervalued, and uncertain about the future of the organization."

Michael explained, "To address this breakdown, leadership implemented a series of measures to improve transparency and foster open dialogue within the organization. Town hall meetings, regular updates, and feedback channels were established to ensure that employees were informed about organizational changes and decisions, and their voices were heard."

The screen displayed images of leaders engaging with employees, sharing insights into organizational strategies and decisions, and soliciting feedback and suggestions. "By prioritizing transparency and open communication, leadership was able to rebuild trust, enhance morale, and create a culture of collaboration and shared purpose within the organization."

Michael continued, "This case study underscores the importance of transparency and honesty in building trust and fostering engagement among employees."

He paused, allowing the significance of the case studies to resonate with the team. "In conclusion," Michael said, turning off the projector and facing his team, "case studies of communication breakdowns and solutions offer us valuable insights into the challenges and opportunities inherent in organizational communication. By learning from these examples and implementing effective solutions, organizations can strengthen their communication practices, build trust, and drive success in an increasingly complex and interconnected world."

With a renewed understanding of the importance of effective communication, the executives at Apex Global Consulting prepared to integrate these lessons into their own management practices, knowing that they held the key to fostering a culture of openness, collaboration, and trust within their organization.

Developing Effective Communication Skills

As the discussion on communication and philosophy continued, Michael shifted the focus towards the practical aspect of developing effective communication skills, recognizing their paramount importance in navigating the complexities of the modern workplace. With anticipation in the air, the executives eagerly awaited to uncover the strategies and techniques that would empower them to become more adept communicators.

"Now, let's explore **developing effective communication skills**," Michael announced, his voice infused with determination and enthusiasm. "Effective communication is not just a desirable trait—it's a fundamental skill that underpins success in management."

He clicked the remote, and the screen illuminated with the title: **"Developing Effective Communication Skills."**

"Our exploration begins with the recognition that communication is both an art and a science—it requires not only knowledge of communication principles but also the development of practical skills and techniques," Michael continued, gesturing towards the screen. "Fortunately, effective communication skills can be cultivated and refined through deliberate practice and commitment."

The screen transitioned to images depicting various aspects of effective communication, from active listening to assertive expression. "Our first consideration is **active listening**. Active listening is the foundation of effective communication—it involves not only hearing what others say but also understanding their perspectives, feelings, and intentions."

Michael explained, "Active listening requires us to be fully present, attentive, and empathetic in our interactions with others. By practicing active listening, we can foster trust, build rapport, and strengthen relationships with colleagues, clients, and stakeholders."

The executives nodded in agreement, recognizing the importance of listening in communication.

"Next," Michael said, clicking to the next slide, "let's explore the art of **assertive communication**. Assertive communication is about expressing our thoughts, feelings, and needs in a clear, confident, and respectful manner."

The screen displayed images of individuals engaging in assertive communication, confidently expressing their ideas and opinions while respecting the perspectives of others. "Assertive communication promotes mutual respect, honesty, and transparency—it allows us to communicate our needs and boundaries effectively, while also respecting the rights and perspectives of others."

Michael continued, "By mastering the art of assertive communication, we can navigate challenging situations, resolve conflicts, and build consensus within our teams and organizations."

The executives leaned forward, captivated by the idea of assertive communication.

"Our final consideration," Michael said, "is the importance of **empathy** in communication. Empathy is the ability to understand and share the feelings of others—it allows us to connect on a deeper level, build trust, and foster collaboration."

The screen transitioned to visuals depicting individuals demonstrating empathy in their communication, acknowledging the emotions and experiences of others with compassion and understanding. "Empathetic communication promotes inclusivity, belonging, and psychological safety—it creates an environment where individuals feel valued, respected, and supported."

Michael explained, "By cultivating empathy in our communication, we can create a culture of trust, collaboration, and innovation within our organizations."

He paused, allowing the significance of effective communication skills to resonate with the team. "In conclusion," Michael said, turning off the projector and facing his team, "developing effective communication skills is essential for success in management. By mastering the art of active listening, assertive communication, and empathy, we can build stronger relationships, resolve conflicts, and drive positive change within our organizations."

With a renewed commitment to developing their communication skills, the executives at Apex Global Consulting prepared to integrate these techniques into their daily interactions, knowing that they held the key to fostering a culture of openness, collaboration, and trust within their organization.

Philosophical Approaches to Conflict Resolution

As the executives delved deeper into the exploration of communication and philosophy, Michael guided their attention towards the profound intersection of philosophical approaches to conflict resolution. With an air of intrigue, they awaited to unravel the timeless wisdom embedded within these philosophical principles.

"Now, let's turn our focus to **philosophical approaches to conflict resolution**," Michael announced, his voice carrying a tone of introspection and contemplation. "Conflict is inevitable in the workplace, but how we address it can make all the difference in fostering a culture of collaboration and growth."

He clicked the remote, and the screen illuminated with the title: **"Philosophical Approaches to Conflict Resolution."**

"Our exploration begins with the recognition that conflict is not inherently negative—it's a natural byproduct of diverse perspectives, goals, and values," Michael continued, gesturing towards the screen. "Philosophical approaches to conflict resolution invite us to transcend the binary notions of 'winning' and 'losing' and instead focus on finding mutually beneficial solutions that honor the dignity and autonomy of all parties involved."

The screen transitioned to images depicting individuals engaged in constructive dialogue, seeking to understand each other's perspectives and find common ground. "Our first consideration is the principle of **dialogue**. Dialogue is the cornerstone of philosophical conflict resolution—it involves open, honest, and respectful communication that seeks to uncover underlying interests, needs, and values."

Michael explained, "By engaging in dialogue, we can move beyond positional bargaining and explore creative solutions that address the root causes of conflict. Dialogue requires active listening, empathy, and a willingness to suspend judgment, as we seek to understand the perspectives and experiences of others."

The executives nodded in agreement, recognizing the transformative power of dialogue in conflict resolution.

"Next," Michael said, clicking to the next slide, "let's explore the principle of **collaboration**. Collaboration is about working together towards shared goals and objectives, leveraging the strengths and perspectives of all parties involved."

The screen displayed images of individuals collaborating to find innovative solutions to complex problems, pooling their resources and expertise to achieve common objectives. "Collaborative conflict resolution promotes inclusivity, creativity, and trust—it acknowledges that everyone has a stake in the outcome and seeks to find solutions that honor the interests and needs of all parties."

Michael continued, "By embracing collaboration, we can transform conflict from a source of division into an opportunity for growth and innovation within our teams and organizations."

The executives leaned forward, captivated by the idea of collaborative conflict resolution.

"Our final consideration," Michael said, "is the principle of **justice**. Justice is about fairness, equity, and respect for the rights and dignity of all parties involved in the conflict."

The screen transitioned to visuals depicting individuals seeking to resolve conflict through the lens of justice, ensuring that outcomes are equitable and respectful of everyone's needs and interests. "Justice-oriented conflict resolution involves identifying underlying power dynamics, addressing structural inequalities, and promoting restorative practices that repair harm and rebuild trust."

Michael explained, "By prioritizing justice in conflict resolution, we can create a culture of fairness, accountability, and respect within our organizations."

He paused, allowing the significance of philosophical approaches to conflict resolution to resonate with the team. "In conclusion," Michael said, turning off the projector and facing his team, "philosophical approaches to conflict resolution offer us valuable insights into transforming conflict from a source of division into an opportunity for growth and collaboration. By embracing principles of dialogue, collaboration, and justice, we can create a culture of openness, trust, and resilience within our organizations."

With a renewed commitment to philosophical conflict resolution, the executives at Apex Global Consulting prepared to apply these principles to their own management practices, knowing that they held the key to fostering a culture of collaboration, innovation, and respect within their organization.

Chapter 12: Innovation and Creativity

Philosophical Insights into Creativity and Innovation

As the executives gathered around the conference table, anticipation filled the air as they prepared to embark on a journey exploring the nexus of innovation and creativity through a philosophical lens. Michael, the facilitator, stood at the front of the room, ready to guide them through the profound insights awaiting discovery.

"Welcome, everyone, to Chapter 12: Innovation and Creativity," Michael began, his voice resonating with enthusiasm and curiosity. "Today, we delve into the philosophical underpinnings that illuminate the nature of creativity and innovation, two pillars essential for organizational success and growth."

He gestured towards the screen, which illuminated with the title: **"Philosophical Insights into Creativity and Innovation."**

"Our exploration begins with the recognition that creativity and innovation are not merely mechanical processes—they are manifestations of the human spirit, expressions of our capacity to imagine, create, and transform the world around us," Michael continued, his words carrying a sense of reverence for the creative impulse.

The screen transitioned to images depicting artists, inventors, and thinkers throughout history, whose groundbreaking ideas and inventions had reshaped society. "Our first consideration is the role of **imagination**. Imagination is the spark that ignites the flames of creativity—it allows us to envision possibilities beyond the constraints of the present reality."

Michael explained, "By tapping into our imagination, we can break free from conventional thinking, challenge assumptions, and envision new possibilities for the future. Imagination is the wellspring of innovation, fueling our quest to explore, experiment, and create."

The executives nodded in agreement, recognizing the transformative power of imagination.

"Next," Michael said, clicking to the next slide, "let's explore the concept of **transformation**. Transformation is the process of turning imaginative ideas into tangible innovations that shape the world around us."

The screen displayed images of innovators and entrepreneurs bringing their ideas to life, from concept sketches to prototype models. "Transformation requires courage, resilience, and a willingness to embrace uncertainty—it's about taking risks, overcoming obstacles, and persevering in the face of adversity."

Michael continued, "By embracing transformation, we can turn dreams into reality, ideas into inventions, and aspirations into achievements. Transformation is the crucible where creativity meets action, where imagination meets reality."

The executives leaned forward, captivated by the idea of transformation through creativity and innovation.

"Our final consideration," Michael said, "is the principle

of **impact**. Impact is the measure of the significance and relevance of our creative endeavors—it's about making a meaningful difference in the lives of others and the world around us."

The screen transitioned to visuals depicting innovations that had transformed industries, revolutionized technologies, and improved the quality of life for countless individuals. "Impact-driven creativity and innovation are guided by a sense of purpose, a commitment to excellence, and a desire to leave a lasting legacy."

Michael explained, "By prioritizing impact in our creative endeavors, we can create a better future for ourselves, our organizations, and our communities. Impact is the legacy we leave behind, the mark we make on the world."

He paused, allowing the significance of philosophical insights into creativity and innovation to resonate with the team. "In conclusion," Michael said, turning off the projector and facing his team, "philosophical insights into creativity and innovation offer us a deeper understanding of the human spirit and its capacity for imagination, transformation, and impact. By embracing these insights, we can unleash our creative potential, cultivate a culture of innovation, and shape a brighter future for ourselves and generations to come."

With a renewed sense of inspiration, the executives at Apex Global Consulting prepared to apply these philosophical insights to their own approach to creativity and innovation, knowing that they held the key to unlocking limitless possibilities for growth and success within their organization.

The Ethics of Innovation

As the executives remained engaged in the exploration of innovation and creativity, Michael directed their attention towards a crucial aspect often overlooked in the pursuit of progress—the ethics of innovation. With an air of solemnity, they awaited to uncover the moral imperatives that underpin the process of innovation.

"Now, let's delve into **the ethics of innovation**," Michael announced, his voice resonating with gravitas and introspection. "Innovation is not just about creating new technologies or products—it's about shaping the future in a way that aligns with our values and principles."

He clicked the remote, and the screen illuminated with the title: **"The Ethics of Innovation."**

"Our exploration begins with the recognition that innovation has the power to both uplift and harm—it can improve lives, drive progress, and solve complex challenges, but it can also exacerbate inequalities, disrupt communities, and pose ethical dilemmas," Michael continued, gesturing towards the screen. "As leaders, it's essential that we consider the ethical implications of our innovative endeavors and ensure that our actions are guided by moral principles and social responsibility."

The screen transitioned to images depicting the dual nature of innovation, from life-saving medical advancements to controversial technologies with potential negative consequences. "Our first consideration is the principle of **beneficence**. Beneficence is the ethical imperative to do good—it requires us to consider the potential benefits and harms of our innovations and prioritize the well-being of individuals and communities."

Michael explained, "By embracing beneficence, we can ensure that our innovations contribute to the greater good, enhance human flourishing, and promote social justice. Beneficence is the moral compass that guides us in navigating the complexities of innovation and ensuring that our actions have a positive impact on society."

The executives nodded in agreement, recognizing the importance of ethical considerations in innovation.

"Next," Michael said, clicking to the next slide, "let's explore the principle of **justice**. Justice is the ethical imperative to ensure fairness, equity, and inclusivity in the distribution of the benefits and burdens of innovation."

The screen displayed images of individuals and communities affected by the consequences of innovation, from marginalized populations disproportionately impacted by technological advancements to workers displaced by automation. "Justice-oriented innovation seeks to address systemic inequalities, mitigate social disparities, and promote access to opportunities for all members of society."

Michael continued, "By prioritizing justice, we can ensure that the benefits of innovation are equitably distributed, and the burdens are borne fairly. Justice is the foundation of a just and inclusive society, where everyone has the opportunity to participate in and benefit from the fruits of innovation."

The executives leaned forward, captivated by the idea of justice-driven innovation.

"Our final consideration," Michael said, "is the principle of **integrity**. Integrity is the ethical imperative to uphold honesty, transparency, and accountability in our innovative endeavors."

The screen transitioned to visuals depicting individuals and organizations demonstrating integrity in their innovation practices, from transparent decision-making processes to honest communication about potential risks and uncertainties. "Integrity-centered innovation fosters trust, credibility, and accountability—it ensures that our actions are guided by ethical principles and that we are accountable for the consequences of our decisions."

Michael explained, "By prioritizing integrity, we can build trust with stakeholders, cultivate a culture of transparency, and uphold the highest ethical standards in our innovation practices."

He paused, allowing the significance of the ethics of innovation to resonate with the team. "In conclusion," Michael said, turning off the projector and facing his team, "the ethics of innovation remind us that with great power comes great responsibility. By embracing principles of beneficence, justice, and integrity, we can ensure that our innovations contribute to a better future for all."

With a renewed commitment to ethical innovation, the executives at Apex Global Consulting prepared to integrate these principles into their own approach to creativity and innovation, knowing that they held the key to shaping a future that is not only innovative but also ethical and just.

Fostering a Culture of Innovation

As the discussion on innovation and ethics settled, Michael shifted the focus towards the practical aspect of fostering a culture of innovation within the organization. With an air of determination, the executives eagerly awaited to uncover the strategies and techniques that would empower them to create an environment where innovation thrived.

"Now, let's explore **fostering a culture of innovation**," Michael announced, his voice infused with determination and enthusiasm. "Creating a culture that embraces innovation is essential for driving progress and staying ahead in today's rapidly evolving world."

He clicked the remote, and the screen illuminated with the title: **"Fostering a Culture of Innovation."**

"Our exploration begins with the recognition that innovation is not just the responsibility of a few—it's a mindset that permeates every level of the organization," Michael continued, gesturing towards the screen. "Fostering a culture of innovation requires leadership commitment, organizational support, and employee engagement."

The screen transitioned to images depicting diverse teams collaborating, brainstorming, and experimenting with new ideas. "Our first consideration is the importance of **leadership support**. Leadership plays a crucial role in setting the tone for innovation—it's about creating a vision, providing resources, and empowering employees to take risks and pursue creative solutions."

Michael explained, "By demonstrating a commitment to innovation, leaders can inspire and motivate employees to think outside the box, challenge the status quo, and pursue bold ideas that drive the organization forward."

The executives nodded in agreement, recognizing the pivotal role of leadership in fostering a culture of innovation.

"Next," Michael said, clicking to the next slide, "let's explore the principle of **organizational support**. Organizational support is about creating structures, processes, and incentives that encourage and reward innovation."

The screen displayed images of innovation labs, cross-functional teams, and dedicated resources for research and development. "Organizational support fosters an environment where creativity and experimentation are encouraged, where failure is seen as a learning opportunity, and where employees feel empowered to take initiative and pursue innovative solutions to complex challenges."

Michael continued, "By providing the necessary resources, training, and support, organizations can create fertile ground for innovation to flourish and thrive."

The executives leaned forward, captivated by the idea of organizational support for innovation.

"Our final consideration," Michael said, "is the importance of **employee engagement**. Employee engagement is about involving employees in the innovation process, soliciting their ideas, and recognizing their contributions."

The screen transitioned to visuals depicting employees actively participating in innovation initiatives, from suggestion programs to innovation competitions. "Employee engagement fosters a sense of ownership, belonging, and pride—it empowers employees to unleash their creative potential, share their insights, and contribute to the organization's success."

Michael explained, "By fostering a culture of openness, collaboration, and trust, organizations can tap into the collective wisdom and creativity of their employees, driving innovation from the bottom up."

He paused, allowing the significance of fostering a culture of innovation to resonate with the team. "In conclusion," Michael said, turning off the projector and facing his team, "fostering a culture of innovation is not just about adopting the latest tools or techniques—it's about creating an environment where creativity, experimentation, and collaboration are valued and encouraged. By embracing leadership support, organizational support, and employee engagement, we can create a culture where innovation thrives and our organization can continue to lead and succeed in a rapidly changing world."

With a renewed commitment to fostering a culture of innovation, the executives at Apex Global Consulting prepared to apply these principles to their own management practices, knowing that they held the key to unlocking limitless possibilities for growth and success within their organization.

Case Studies of Innovative Companies

As the executives immersed themselves in the exploration of fostering a culture of innovation, Michael turned their attention to real-world examples of companies that had successfully embraced innovation. With a sense of anticipation, they eagerly awaited to uncover the strategies and insights behind these innovative organizations.

"Now, let's delve into **case studies of innovative companies**," Michael announced, his voice filled with excitement and curiosity. "Studying the experiences of other organizations can provide valuable insights and inspiration for fostering innovation within our own company."

He clicked the remote, and the screen illuminated with the title: **"Case Studies of Innovative Companies."**

"Our exploration begins with the recognition that innovation can take many forms and can emerge from unexpected sources," Michael continued, gesturing towards the screen. "By studying the experiences of innovative companies, we can gain a deeper understanding of the strategies, practices, and cultures that foster creativity and drive success."

The screen transitioned to images depicting renowned companies known for their innovative achievements, from tech giants to startups disrupting traditional industries. "Our first case study is **Apple Inc.** Apple's commitment to innovation has been a cornerstone of its success—from the revolutionary products like the iPhone and iPad to its innovative retail stores and marketing campaigns."

Michael explained, "Apple's culture of innovation is characterized by a relentless focus on customer experience, a passion for design excellence, and a willingness to take risks and challenge conventional wisdom. By embracing a culture of innovation, Apple has transformed industries, redefined markets, and created iconic products that have become integral parts of our lives."

The executives nodded in agreement, recognizing the transformative impact of Apple's innovation.

"Next," Michael said, clicking to the next slide, "let's explore the case of **Google**. Google's commitment to innovation extends beyond its core search engine to a wide range of products and services, from self-driving cars to artificial intelligence and cloud computing."

The screen displayed images of Google's innovative projects and initiatives, from its moonshot projects at Google X to its open and collaborative work environment. "Google's culture of innovation is characterized by a spirit of experimentation, a willingness to fail fast and iterate, and a focus on solving big, complex problems that have the potential to change the world."

Michael continued, "By fostering a culture where employees

are encouraged to think creatively, take risks, and pursue ambitious goals, Google has become synonymous with innovation and has positioned itself as a leader in the technology industry."

The executives leaned forward, captivated by the innovative practices of Google.

"Our final case study," Michael said, "is the story of **Tesla**. Tesla's vision of accelerating the world's transition to sustainable energy has driven its innovative approach to electric vehicles, renewable energy, and energy storage solutions."

The screen transitioned to visuals depicting Tesla's groundbreaking products and initiatives, from its electric vehicles to its solar panels and batteries. "Tesla's culture of innovation is rooted in a commitment to sustainability, a passion for disruptive innovation, and a willingness to challenge the status quo of the automotive industry."

Michael explained, "By pushing the boundaries of technology, embracing risk-taking, and prioritizing long-term goals over short-term gains, Tesla has revolutionized the automotive industry, inspired a new wave of innovation, and paved the way for a more sustainable future."

He paused, allowing the significance of the case studies of innovative companies to resonate with the team. "In conclusion," Michael said, turning off the projector and facing his team, "by studying the experiences of innovative companies like Apple, Google, and Tesla, we can gain valuable insights and inspiration for fostering a culture of innovation within our own organization. By embracing their strategies, practices, and cultures, we can unlock the creative potential of our teams, drive progress, and achieve success in a rapidly changing world."

With a renewed sense of inspiration, the executives at Apex

Global Consulting prepared to apply the lessons learned from these case studies to their own approach to fostering a culture of innovation, knowing that they held the key to unlocking limitless possibilities for growth and success within their organization.

Balancing Risk and Innovation

As the executives continued their exploration of fostering innovation, Michael shifted their focus towards a critical aspect often overlooked in the pursuit of progress—the delicate balance between risk and innovation. With a sense of urgency, they awaited to uncover the strategies and insights that would empower them to navigate this intricate interplay.

"Now, let's delve into **balancing risk and innovation**," Michael announced, his voice laced with determination and contemplation. "Innovation requires taking risks, but managing those risks effectively is essential for long-term success and sustainability."

He clicked the remote, and the screen illuminated with the title: **"Balancing Risk and Innovation."**

"Our exploration begins with the recognition that innovation inherently involves uncertainty and the possibility of failure," Michael continued, gesturing towards the screen. "By understanding and managing the risks associated with innovation, we can minimize potential negative outcomes and maximize the likelihood of success."

The screen transitioned to images depicting the dynamic relationship between risk and innovation, from calculated risks that lead to breakthrough innovations to unchecked risks that result in failure. "Our first consideration is the importance of **risk assessment**. Before embarking on any innovative endeavor, it's crucial to conduct a thorough assessment of the potential risks and rewards."

Michael explained, "By identifying and evaluating the risks associated with an innovation project, organizations can make informed decisions about resource allocation, project prioritization, and risk mitigation strategies. Risk assessment provides a roadmap for navigating uncertainty and maximizing the chances of success."

The executives nodded in agreement, recognizing the importance of risk assessment in innovation.

"Next," Michael said, clicking to the next slide, "let's explore the principle of **risk tolerance**. Risk tolerance is about understanding the organization's appetite for risk and aligning innovation efforts with its strategic objectives and risk management policies."

The screen displayed images of organizations with varying degrees of risk tolerance, from conservative approaches that prioritize stability and predictability to bold strategies that embrace uncertainty and disruption. "By defining and communicating clear risk tolerance levels, organizations can create a culture where innovation is encouraged, but risks are managed responsibly."

Michael continued, "By striking the right balance between risk and reward, organizations can unleash their creative potential, drive progress, and achieve sustainable growth."

The executives leaned forward, captivated by the idea of balancing risk and innovation.

"Our final consideration," Michael said, "is the importance of **risk mitigation**. Risk mitigation involves identifying potential risks, developing strategies to minimize their likelihood and impact, and implementing controls to monitor and manage risks throughout the innovation process."

The screen transitioned to visuals depicting risk mitigation strategies, from diversifying innovation portfolios to establishing contingency plans and fallback options. "By proactively addressing potential risks, organizations can reduce the likelihood of failure, protect their investments, and increase their resilience in the face of uncertainty."

Michael explained, "By embracing a culture of risk-aware innovation and implementing robust risk management practices, organizations can navigate the complexities of innovation with confidence and achieve sustainable success."

He paused, allowing the significance of balancing risk and innovation to resonate with the team. "In conclusion," Michael said, turning off the projector and facing his team, "balancing risk and innovation is about embracing uncertainty while also managing it effectively. By conducting risk assessments, defining risk tolerance levels, and implementing risk mitigation strategies, we can foster a culture where innovation thrives, risks are managed responsibly, and success is achieved sustainably."

With a renewed commitment to balancing risk and innovation, the executives at Apex Global Consulting prepared to apply these principles to their own approach to fostering innovation, knowing that they held the key to unlocking limitless possibilities for growth and success within their organization.

Tools for Encouraging Creative Thinking

As the discussion on balancing risk and innovation settled, Michael directed the executives' attention towards practical tools and techniques for encouraging creative thinking within the organization. With a sense of anticipation, they eagerly awaited to uncover the strategies that would empower them to foster a culture of creativity and innovation.

"Now, let's explore **tools for encouraging creative thinking**," Michael announced, his voice filled with enthusiasm and anticipation. "Creativity is the lifeblood of innovation, and providing employees with the right tools and techniques can unleash their creative potential and drive progress."

He clicked the remote, and the screen illuminated with the title: "**Tools for Encouraging Creative Thinking.**"

"Our exploration begins with the recognition that creativity is not just a talent—it's a skill that can be cultivated and nurtured," Michael continued, gesturing towards the screen. "By providing employees with tools and techniques to stimulate their creativity, organizations can create an environment where innovation flourishes and breakthrough ideas emerge."

The screen transitioned to images depicting various tools and techniques for encouraging creative thinking, from brainstorming sessions to design thinking workshops. "Our first tool is **brainstorming**. Brainstorming is a collaborative technique that encourages participants to generate a wide range of ideas, without judgment or criticism."

Michael explained, "By creating a safe space for employees to share their ideas freely, brainstorming can stimulate creativity, foster collaboration, and uncover innovative solutions to complex problems."

The executives nodded in agreement, recognizing the power of brainstorming in unlocking creative potential.

"Next," Michael said, clicking to the next slide, "let's explore the technique of **mind mapping**. Mind mapping is a visual tool that allows individuals to organize their thoughts, ideas, and associations in a non-linear format."

The screen displayed examples of mind maps, with colorful branches representing different ideas and connections. "Mind mapping encourages divergent thinking, stimulates creativity, and helps individuals explore new perspectives and connections that may not be immediately apparent."

Michael continued, "By incorporating mind mapping into their creative process, individuals can unleash their imagination, overcome mental barriers, and generate innovative ideas."

The executives leaned forward, captivated by the idea of using mind maps to enhance their creative thinking.

"Our final tool," Michael said, "is the technique of **design thinking**. Design thinking is a human-centered approach to problem-solving that emphasizes empathy, creativity, and experimentation."

The screen transitioned to visuals depicting the stages of the design thinking process, from empathizing with users to prototyping and testing solutions. "Design thinking encourages a holistic understanding of the problem, fosters collaboration across disciplines, and empowers teams to iterate rapidly and innovate iteratively."

Michael explained, "By embracing design thinking, organizations can gain deeper insights into user needs, identify new opportunities for innovation, and develop solutions that are truly transformative and impactful."

He paused, allowing the significance of tools for encouraging creative thinking to resonate with the team. "In conclusion," Michael said, turning off the projector and facing his team, "by providing employees with tools and techniques such as brainstorming, mind mapping, and design thinking, organizations can unlock their creative potential, drive innovation, and achieve success in a rapidly changing world."

With a renewed commitment to encouraging creative thinking, the executives at Apex Global Consulting prepared to integrate these tools into their own approach to fostering innovation, knowing that they held the key to unlocking limitless possibilities for growth and success within their organization.

Chapter 13: Power and Authority in Management

Philosophical Theories of Power and Authority

As the executives settled in for their next discussion, Michael shifted their attention towards the intricate dynamics of power and authority within the realm of management. With a sense of gravitas, they awaited to delve into the philosophical underpinnings that governed these fundamental aspects of organizational leadership.

"Now, let's embark on the exploration of **power and authority in management**," Michael announced, his voice carrying a tone of introspection and inquiry. "Understanding the philosophical theories that underpin these concepts is crucial for effective leadership and organizational governance."

He clicked the remote, and the screen illuminated with the title: **"Philosophical Theories of Power and Authority."**

"Our journey begins with the recognition that power and authority are not merely hierarchical structures, but complex constructs deeply rooted in philosophical thought," Michael continued, gesturing towards the screen. "By examining these theories, we can gain insights into the nature of power, the legitimacy of authority, and the ethical implications of leadership."

The screen transitioned to images depicting influential philosophers and their theories on power and authority, from Plato and Aristotle to Machiavelli and Weber. "Our first consideration is the concept of **natural law**. Natural law theorists, such as Aristotle, argued that power and authority derive from inherent qualities or principles that govern the universe."

Michael explained, "According to natural law theory, leaders derive their authority from their adherence to moral principles, their ability to promote the common good, and their alignment with the natural order of things. Natural law provides a foundation for ethical leadership and serves as a guide for determining the legitimacy of authority."

The executives nodded in agreement, recognizing the timeless relevance of natural law in shaping principles of leadership.

"Next," Michael said, clicking to the next slide, "let's explore the theory of **social contract**. Social contract theorists, such as Hobbes and Rousseau, argued that power and authority are based on agreements or contracts between individuals and the governing institutions."

The screen displayed images depicting the social contract as a foundational principle of modern governance, from the Magna Carta to constitutional democracies. "According to social contract theory, individuals consent to be governed in exchange for protection of their rights and freedoms. Leaders derive their authority from the consent of the governed and are accountable to the people they serve."

Michael continued, "Social contract theory provides a

framework for understanding the relationship between rulers and the ruled, and the obligations and responsibilities that come with positions of power."

The executives leaned forward, captivated by the implications of social contract theory for modern leadership.

"Our final consideration," Michael said, "is the concept of **legitimacy**. Legitimacy refers to the perceived rightfulness or validity of authority, and it is essential for maintaining stability and order within organizations and societies."

The screen transitioned to visuals depicting various sources of legitimacy, from tradition and charisma to legal-rational authority. "Legitimacy is often derived from tradition, where authority is passed down through hereditary or cultural means. Alternatively, legitimacy can stem from charisma, where leaders inspire trust and loyalty through their personal qualities and magnetism."

Michael explained, "By understanding the sources of legitimacy, leaders can cultivate trust, build credibility, and foster a sense of legitimacy among their followers."

He paused, allowing the significance of philosophical theories of power and authority to resonate with the team. "In conclusion," Michael said, turning off the projector and facing his team, "by examining philosophical theories of power and authority, we can gain deeper insights into the nature of leadership, the dynamics of governance, and the ethical considerations that guide our actions as leaders. By embracing principles of natural law, social contract, and legitimacy, we can cultivate a leadership style that is ethical, accountable, and effective in driving organizational success."

With a renewed understanding of the philosophical foundations of power and authority, the executives at Apex Global

Consulting prepared to apply these insights to their own approach to leadership and management, knowing that they held the key to shaping a future that is not only successful but also ethically grounded and morally responsible.

Ethical Use of Power in Organizations

As the executives delved deeper into the discussion on power and authority in management, Michael redirected their attention towards the ethical dimensions of wielding power within organizational contexts. With a sense of urgency, they awaited to explore the principles that would guide them in using power responsibly and ethically.

"Now, let's turn our focus towards **the ethical use of power in organizations**," Michael declared, his voice carrying a tone of solemn reflection and moral inquiry. "While power can be a force for positive change, its ethical use is essential for fostering trust, promoting fairness, and upholding integrity within our organizations."

He clicked the remote, and the screen illuminated with the title: **"Ethical Use of Power in Organizations."**

"Our exploration begins with the recognition that power, when wielded ethically, can be a force for good," Michael continued, gesturing towards the screen. "By examining the ethical principles that govern the use of power, we can ensure that our actions as leaders align with our values and contribute to the greater good."

The screen transitioned to images depicting ethical leaders and their principles of ethical leadership, from transparency and accountability to empathy and fairness. "Our first consideration is the principle of **transparency**. Transparency requires leaders to be open and honest in their communication and decision-making, ensuring that information is shared openly and that decisions are made with integrity."

Michael explained, "By promoting transparency, leaders can build trust, foster collaboration, and empower employees to make informed decisions. Transparency also serves as a safeguard against abuse of power and unethical behavior."

The executives nodded in agreement, recognizing the importance of transparency in maintaining ethical standards.

"Next," Michael said, clicking to the next slide, "let's explore the principle of **accountability**. Accountability requires leaders to take responsibility for their actions and to be answerable to others for the consequences of those actions."

The screen displayed images depicting leaders holding themselves and others accountable for their behavior and decisions. "By promoting accountability, leaders demonstrate their commitment to ethical behavior, ensure that standards are upheld, and provide a mechanism for addressing wrongdoing and restoring trust."

Michael continued, "Accountability also serves as a deterrent against abuse of power and unethical behavior, creating a culture where integrity and ethical conduct are valued and rewarded."

The executives leaned forward, captivated by the implications of accountability for ethical leadership.

"Our final consideration," Michael said, "is the principle of **fairness**. Fairness requires leaders to treat all individuals with respect, dignity, and equity, regardless of their status or position within the organization."

The screen transitioned to visuals depicting leaders promoting fairness through inclusive decision-making processes and equitable distribution of resources. "By promoting fairness, leaders create a culture of trust, respect, and collaboration, where all individuals feel valued and empowered to contribute their best."

Michael explained, "Fairness also serves as a safeguard against favoritism, discrimination, and abuse of power, ensuring that decisions are made impartially and in the best interests of the organization and its stakeholders."

He paused, allowing the significance of the ethical use of power in organizations to resonate with the team. "In conclusion," Michael said, turning off the projector and facing his team, "by embracing principles of transparency, accountability, and fairness, we can wield power ethically and responsibly, fostering a culture of trust, integrity, and ethical conduct within our organizations. By upholding these principles, we can ensure that our actions as leaders contribute to the greater good and create a positive impact on our employees, stakeholders, and society at large."

With a renewed commitment to ethical leadership, the executives at Apex Global Consulting prepared to integrate these principles into their own approach to wielding power within their organization, knowing that they held the key to shaping a future that is not only successful but also morally upright and ethically sound.

Leadership and Authority: A Philosophical Approach

As the discussion on power and authority continued, Michael guided the executives towards a deeper exploration of leadership and its philosophical underpinnings. With a sense of anticipation, they eagerly awaited to uncover the timeless wisdom that would illuminate their understanding of leadership and authority within organizational contexts.

"Now, let's delve into **leadership and authority: a philosophical approach**," Michael declared, his voice resonating with a tone of reverence and intellectual curiosity. "By examining leadership through a philosophical lens, we can gain profound insights into the nature of leadership, its ethical dimensions, and its transformative potential."

He clicked the remote, and the screen illuminated with the title: "**Leadership and Authority: A Philosophical Approach.**"

"Our journey begins with the recognition that leadership is more than just a position or title—it's a moral and philosophical endeavor," Michael continued, gesturing towards the screen. "By exploring the philosophical foundations of leadership, we can cultivate a deeper understanding of its essence and its implications for organizational governance."

The screen transitioned to images depicting influential philosophers and their perspectives on leadership, from Plato and Aristotle to Kant and Nietzsche. "Our first consideration is the concept of **virtue ethics**. Virtue ethics emphasizes the importance of character, integrity, and moral excellence in leadership."

Michael explained, "According to virtue ethics, effective leadership requires cultivating virtues such as courage, wisdom, compassion, and justice. By embodying these virtues, leaders inspire trust, foster collaboration, and promote the common good."

The executives nodded in agreement, recognizing the timeless wisdom of virtue ethics in shaping principles of leadership.

"Next," Michael said, clicking to the next slide, "let's explore the philosophy of **servant leadership**. Servant leadership is rooted in the idea that leaders exist to serve others, rather than to exert power or control over them."

The screen displayed images depicting leaders serving their followers with humility, empathy, and compassion. "According to servant leadership, leaders prioritize the needs of others, empower their teams, and create conditions for personal and professional growth. By serving others selflessly, leaders earn the trust and loyalty of their followers and foster a culture of collaboration and mutual respect."

Michael continued, "Servant leadership is not about wielding authority, but about empowering others to reach their full potential and achieve collective goals."

The executives leaned forward, captivated by the idea of servant leadership as a transformative approach to leadership.

"Our final consideration," Michael said, "is the philosophy of **transformational leadership**. Transformational leadership is based on the idea that leaders inspire and motivate their followers to achieve extraordinary results through vision, charisma, and intellectual stimulation."

The screen transitioned to visuals depicting transformational leaders inspiring change and innovation within their organizations. "According to transformational leadership, leaders inspire their teams by articulating a compelling vision, fostering a sense of purpose and belonging, and challenging them to think creatively and embrace change."

Michael explained, "By adopting a transformational approach to leadership, leaders can unleash the potential of their teams, drive innovation, and achieve breakthrough results."

He paused, allowing the significance of leadership and

authority from a philosophical approach to resonate with the team. "In conclusion," Michael said, turning off the projector and facing his team, "by examining leadership through a philosophical lens, we can gain deeper insights into its essence, its ethical dimensions, and its transformative potential. By embracing principles of virtue ethics, servant leadership, and transformational leadership, we can cultivate a leadership style that is ethical, inspirational, and effective in driving organizational success."

With a renewed understanding of leadership from a philosophical perspective, the executives at Apex Global Consulting prepared to integrate these insights into their own approach to leadership and authority, knowing that they held the key to shaping a future that is not only successful but also morally upright and ethically sound.

Case Studies of Power Dynamics in Business

As the executives continued their exploration of power and authority, Michael directed their attention towards real-world examples of power dynamics in business. With a sense of intrigue, they eagerly awaited to uncover the complexities and nuances of power relations within organizational contexts.

"Now, let's examine **case studies of power dynamics in business**," Michael declared, his voice tinged with anticipation and intellectual curiosity. "By analyzing these case studies, we can gain practical insights into the complexities of power and authority in organizational settings."

He clicked the remote, and the screen illuminated with the title: **"Case Studies of Power Dynamics in Business."**

"Our journey begins with the recognition that power dynamics permeate every aspect of organizational life," Michael continued, gesturing towards the screen. "By examining these case studies, we can understand how power is wielded, negotiated, and contested within businesses, and the impact it has on individuals, teams, and the organization as a whole."

The screen transitioned to images depicting scenarios of power struggles, influence tactics, and leadership dynamics in various business contexts. "Our first case study examines a scenario of **leadership succession**. In this case, a long-standing CEO retires, leaving a power vacuum and triggering a struggle for control among senior executives and board members."

Michael explained, "This case study illustrates how power dynamics can intensify during times of transition, as individuals jockey for position and influence. It also highlights the importance of effective succession planning and leadership development in mitigating power struggles and ensuring organizational continuity."

The executives nodded in agreement, recognizing the relevance of leadership succession in shaping power dynamics within organizations.

"Next," Michael said, clicking to the next slide, "let's explore a case study of **organizational culture**. In this scenario, a company experiences a cultural shift following a merger or acquisition, as employees from different organizational cultures clash over values, norms, and ways of working."

The screen displayed images depicting employees grappling with change, uncertainty, and conflicting expectations. "This case study illustrates how power dynamics can manifest in the form of cultural clashes, resistance to change, and struggles for influence within organizations undergoing transformation. It also underscores the importance of effective communication, leadership alignment, and cultural integration in navigating such challenges."

Michael continued, "By addressing cultural differences proactively and fostering a culture of collaboration and inclusion, organizations can mitigate power struggles and create a more cohesive and resilient workforce."

The executives leaned forward, captivated by the complexities of organizational culture and its implications for power dynamics.

"Our final case study," Michael said, "examines a scenario of **ethical dilemmas**. In this case, a company faces allegations of unethical behavior, such as fraud, corruption, or environmental misconduct, leading to public outcry, legal scrutiny, and reputational damage."

The screen transitioned to visuals depicting the fallout from ethical lapses, including damaged trust, lost credibility, and financial losses. "This case study highlights how power dynamics can influence ethical decision-making within organizations, as leaders balance competing interests and navigate conflicting priorities. It also underscores the importance of ethical leadership, accountability, and transparency in maintaining organizational integrity and trust."

Michael explained, "By promoting a culture of ethical conduct and holding individuals accountable for their actions, organizations can prevent ethical lapses, mitigate reputational risks, and uphold their commitment to responsible business practices."

He paused, allowing the significance of case studies of power dynamics in business to resonate with the team. "In conclusion," Michael said, turning off the projector and facing his team, "by analyzing these case studies, we can gain practical insights into the complexities of power and authority in organizational settings. By addressing leadership succession, organizational culture, and ethical dilemmas proactively, we can foster a culture of trust, collaboration, and ethical conduct within our organizations. By learning from these examples, we can navigate power dynamics effectively and lead our organizations towards sustainable success."

With a renewed understanding of power dynamics in business, the executives at Apex Global Consulting prepared to apply these insights to their own leadership practices, knowing that they held the key to shaping a future that is not only successful but also ethical, resilient, and morally responsible.

Strategies for Ethical Management of Power

As the executives continued their exploration of power dynamics, Michael steered the conversation towards practical strategies for ethical management of power within organizations. With a sense of purpose, they eagerly awaited to uncover actionable approaches that would enable them to navigate power dynamics with integrity and responsibility.

"Now, let's discuss **strategies for ethical management of power**," Michael declared, his voice resonating with a tone of determination and resolve. "By implementing these strategies, we can ensure that power is wielded responsibly, ethically, and in the best interests of our organizations and stakeholders."

He clicked the remote, and the screen illuminated with the title: **"Strategies for Ethical Management of Power."**

"Our journey begins with the recognition that ethical management of power requires a proactive approach and a commitment to upholding principles of integrity, fairness, and accountability," Michael continued, gesturing towards the screen. "By adopting these strategies, we can promote a culture of ethical conduct, trust, and transparency within our organizations."

The screen transitioned to images depicting leaders implementing various strategies for ethical management of power, from setting clear expectations to fostering a culture of openness and accountability. "Our first strategy is **setting clear expectations**. Leaders must establish clear guidelines, policies, and expectations regarding the use of power and authority within the organization."

Michael explained, "By communicating expectations clearly and consistently, leaders provide guidance for ethical conduct and ensure that employees understand their rights, responsibilities, and the consequences of their actions."

The executives nodded in agreement, recognizing the importance of setting clear expectations in promoting ethical behavior.

"Next," Michael said, clicking to the next slide, "let's explore the strategy of **fostering a culture of openness and accountability**. Leaders must create an environment where individuals feel empowered to speak up, raise concerns, and hold themselves and others accountable for their actions."

The screen displayed images depicting leaders encouraging transparency, honesty, and constructive feedback within their organizations. "By fostering a culture of openness and accountability, leaders create a climate of trust, respect, and collaboration, where ethical behavior is valued and rewarded."

Michael continued, "Leaders must lead by example, demonstrating integrity, humility, and a willingness to admit mistakes and learn from them. By promoting open communication and accountability, leaders can prevent abuses of power, address issues proactively, and maintain the trust and confidence of their teams."

The executives leaned forward, captivated by the idea of fostering a culture of openness and accountability as a cornerstone of ethical leadership.

"Our final strategy," Michael said, "is **providing training and support**. Leaders must equip employees with the knowledge, skills, and resources they need to navigate power dynamics effectively and ethically."

The screen transitioned to visuals depicting leaders providing training on ethical decision-making, conflict resolution, and communication skills. "By investing in training and support, leaders empower employees to make ethical choices, resolve conflicts constructively, and navigate complex power dynamics with confidence and integrity."

Michael explained, "Leaders must provide ongoing support, guidance, and mentorship to employees, helping them develop the resilience, courage, and moral character needed to uphold ethical standards in the face of challenges and temptations."

He paused, allowing the significance of strategies for ethical management of power to resonate with the team. "In conclusion," Michael said, turning off the projector and facing his team, "by implementing these strategies, we can promote a culture of ethical conduct, trust, and transparency within our organizations. By setting clear expectations, fostering a culture of openness and accountability, and providing training and support, we can navigate power dynamics responsibly and lead our organizations towards sustainable success."

With a renewed commitment to ethical management of

power, the executives at Apex Global Consulting prepared to implement these strategies within their own organization, knowing that they held the key to fostering a culture of integrity, trust, and ethical conduct.

Developing Authority through Wisdom and Integrity

As the executives continued their exploration of power and authority, Michael guided their attention towards the development of authority through wisdom and integrity. With a sense of reverence, they eagerly awaited to uncover the transformative potential of embodying these virtues in their leadership roles.

"Now, let's delve into **developing authority through wisdom and integrity**," Michael declared, his voice echoing with a tone of solemn reflection and moral aspiration. "By embracing these virtues, we can cultivate a form of authority that is grounded in ethical principles, respected by others, and conducive to positive change within our organizations."

He clicked the remote, and the screen illuminated with the title: "**Developing Authority through Wisdom and Integrity.**"

"Our journey begins with the recognition that authority, when wielded wisely and with integrity, can inspire trust, foster collaboration, and drive meaningful change," Michael continued, gesturing towards the screen. "By developing authority through wisdom and integrity, we can become ethical leaders who lead by example and earn the respect and admiration of our teams."

The screen transitioned to images depicting leaders embodying wisdom and integrity in their actions and decisions, from making difficult choices with clarity and foresight to upholding moral principles even in the face of adversity. "Our first consideration is the virtue of **wisdom**. Wisdom is the ability to make sound judgments, exercise discernment, and apply knowledge and experience to navigate complex situations effectively."

Michael explained, "By cultivating wisdom, leaders can make informed decisions, anticipate challenges, and chart a course of action that aligns with the organization's values and goals. Wisdom enables leaders to see the bigger picture, identify opportunities for growth and innovation, and guide their teams towards success."

The executives nodded in agreement, recognizing the importance of wisdom in leadership development.

"Next," Michael said, clicking to the next slide, "let's explore the virtue of **integrity**. Integrity is the foundation of ethical leadership, encompassing honesty, transparency, and consistency in word and deed."

The screen displayed images depicting leaders demonstrating integrity through their actions, from honoring commitments and upholding promises to admitting mistakes and taking responsibility for their actions. "By embodying integrity, leaders build trust, credibility, and respect among their teams and stakeholders."

Michael continued, "Integrity is not just about following rules or adhering to codes of conduct—it's about doing what is right, even when no one is watching. Leaders who demonstrate integrity inspire others to do the same, fostering a culture of honesty, accountability, and ethical conduct within their organizations."

The executives leaned forward, captivated by the idea of

developing authority through wisdom and integrity as a path towards ethical leadership.

"Our final consideration," Michael said, "is the synergy between wisdom and integrity in the development of authority. Wisdom without integrity can lead to exploitation and abuse of power, while integrity without wisdom can result in well-intentioned but misguided actions."

The screen transitioned to visuals depicting the interplay between wisdom and integrity in leadership, highlighting the importance of balancing these virtues in ethical decision-making and behavior. "By cultivating both wisdom and integrity, leaders can develop a form of authority that is grounded in ethical principles, respected by others, and conducive to positive change within their organizations."

Michael explained, "Leaders who embody wisdom and integrity lead with humility, empathy, and a commitment to serving the greater good. They inspire trust, foster collaboration, and empower their teams to reach their full potential."

He paused, allowing the significance of developing authority through wisdom and integrity to resonate with the team. "In conclusion," Michael said, turning off the projector and facing his team, "by embracing the virtues of wisdom and integrity, we can cultivate a form of authority that is ethical, respected, and transformative. By leading with wisdom and integrity, we can inspire trust, foster collaboration, and drive meaningful change within our organizations and beyond."

With a renewed commitment to developing authority through wisdom and integrity, the executives at Apex Global Consulting prepared to embody these virtues in their leadership roles, knowing that they held the key to shaping a future that is not only successful but also ethical, compassionate, and morally upright.

Chapter 14: Globalization and Management

Philosophical Perspectives on Globalization

As the executives gathered in the boardroom, Michael began the discussion on globalization and management, setting the stage for a journey into the philosophical perspectives that underpin this complex phenomenon.

"Welcome, everyone, to our discussion on **globalization and management**," Michael began, his voice carrying a tone of anticipation and intellectual curiosity. "Today, we will explore how globalization reshapes the landscape of management and organizations, and the philosophical insights that can guide us in navigating this interconnected world."

He clicked the remote, and the screen illuminated with the title: **"Philosophical Perspectives on Globalization."**

"Our journey begins with the recognition that globalization is more than just economic integration—it's a multifaceted process that shapes cultures, societies, and organizations in profound ways," Michael continued, gesturing towards the screen. "By examining globalization through a philosophical lens, we can gain deeper insights into its nature, dynamics, and implications for management."

The screen transitioned to images depicting the interconnectedness of the global economy, cultural exchange, and technological advancements. "Our first consideration is the philosophical perspective of **cosmopolitanism**. Cosmopolitanism emphasizes the idea that we are citizens of the world, bound by a common humanity and interconnectedness that transcends national borders and cultural differences."

Michael explained, "By embracing cosmopolitanism, organizations can foster a sense of global citizenship, promote cross-cultural understanding, and leverage diversity as a source of innovation and creativity. Cosmopolitanism encourages us to transcend parochialism and ethnocentrism, and to embrace a broader perspective that recognizes the interconnectedness of our world."

The executives nodded in agreement, recognizing the relevance of cosmopolitanism in an increasingly interconnected world.

"Next," Michael said, clicking to the next slide, "let's explore the philosophy of **global justice**. Global justice addresses the ethical challenges of globalization, including inequalities in wealth and power, environmental degradation, and human rights violations."

The screen displayed images depicting global inequalities, environmental destruction, and humanitarian crises. "Global justice calls for a more equitable distribution of resources, opportunities, and benefits of globalization, and recognizes the responsibilities of individuals, organizations, and governments towards addressing global challenges."

Michael continued, "By embracing principles of global

justice, organizations can contribute to a more just and sustainable world, by promoting fair labor practices, environmental sustainability, and social responsibility in their global operations."

The executives leaned forward, captivated by the idea of global justice as a guiding principle for responsible globalization.

"Our final consideration," Michael said, "is the philosophy of **cultural relativism**. Cultural relativism emphasizes the importance of respecting cultural diversity and recognizing the validity of different cultural norms, values, and practices."

The screen transitioned to visuals depicting cultural diversity and the richness of human experience around the world. "Cultural relativism challenges us to question our own cultural assumptions and biases, and to approach cross-cultural interactions with humility, curiosity, and empathy."

Michael explained, "By embracing cultural relativism, organizations can foster inclusive workplaces, build trust and collaboration across cultural boundaries, and harness the potential of cultural diversity as a source of innovation and creativity."

He paused, allowing the significance of philosophical perspectives on globalization to resonate with the team. "In conclusion," Michael said, turning off the projector and facing his team, "by examining globalization through a philosophical lens, we can gain deeper insights into its nature, dynamics, and implications for management. By embracing cosmopolitanism, global justice, and cultural relativism, we can navigate globalization responsibly, ethically, and sustainably, and lead our organizations towards success in an interconnected world."

With a renewed understanding of globalization from a philosophical perspective, the executives at Apex Global Consulting prepared to integrate these insights into their management practices, knowing that they held the key to shaping a future that is not only successful but also ethical, inclusive, and globally responsible.

Ethical Challenges in Global Business

As the discussion on globalization and management progressed, Michael directed the executives' attention towards the ethical challenges that accompany global business operations. With a sense of urgency, they prepared to confront these challenges head-on, armed with the wisdom of philosophical perspectives.

"Now, let's turn our focus to **ethical challenges in global business**," Michael declared, his voice tinged with solemnity and determination. "As organizations expand their operations across borders, they encounter a myriad of ethical dilemmas that require careful consideration and principled decision-making."

He clicked the remote, and the screen illuminated with the title: **"Ethical Challenges in Global Business."**

"Our journey continues with the recognition that global business operations bring with them a host of ethical challenges, ranging from human rights violations to environmental degradation," Michael continued, gesturing towards the screen. "By examining these challenges through a philosophical lens, we can develop strategies to navigate them responsibly and ethically."

The screen transitioned to images depicting scenes of labor

exploitation, environmental pollution, and corruption in global business contexts. "Our first consideration is the challenge of **labor rights**. In many parts of the world, workers are subjected to exploitative labor practices, including low wages, long hours, and unsafe working conditions."

Michael explained, "Organizations must ensure that their global supply chains adhere to ethical labor standards and respect the rights and dignity of workers. This requires transparency, accountability, and collaboration with stakeholders to address systemic issues such as forced labor, child labor, and discrimination."

The executives nodded in agreement, recognizing the importance of upholding labor rights in global business operations.

"Next," Michael said, clicking to the next slide, "let's explore the challenge of **environmental sustainability**. Global business activities often have significant environmental impacts, including pollution, deforestation, and climate change."

The screen displayed images depicting environmental degradation and its consequences for ecosystems and communities. "Organizations must adopt sustainable business practices that minimize their environmental footprint and promote ecological stewardship."

Michael continued, "This requires integrating environmental considerations into business decision-making, investing in renewable energy, reducing waste and emissions, and collaborating with partners to address global environmental challenges."

The executives leaned forward, captivated by the urgency of addressing environmental sustainability in global business operations.

"Our final consideration," Michael said, "is the challenge

of **corruption and bribery**. In many parts of the world, corruption is endemic, posing significant ethical and legal risks for organizations operating globally."

The screen transitioned to visuals depicting instances of bribery, extortion, and unethical business practices. "Organizations must implement robust anti-corruption measures, including clear policies, training programs, and oversight mechanisms to prevent bribery and corruption."

Michael explained, "By fostering a culture of integrity, transparency, and accountability, organizations can mitigate the risk of corruption and uphold ethical standards in their global operations."

He paused, allowing the significance of ethical challenges in global business to resonate with the team. "In conclusion," Michael said, turning off the projector and facing his team, "by examining these ethical challenges through a philosophical lens, we can develop strategies to navigate them responsibly and ethically. By upholding labor rights, promoting environmental sustainability, and combating corruption, we can ensure that our global business operations are conducted with integrity, respect, and accountability."

With a renewed commitment to ethical conduct in global business, the executives at Apex Global Consulting prepared to implement these strategies within their own organization, knowing that they held the key to shaping a future that is not only successful but also ethical, sustainable, and socially responsible.

Cross-cultural Management Philosophies

As the executives delved deeper into the complexities of globalization and management, Michael shifted their focus towards understanding the nuances of cross-cultural management philosophies. With a sense of anticipation, they prepared to explore the rich tapestry of cultural diversity and its implications for organizational success.

"Now, let's explore **cross-cultural management philosophies**," Michael declared, his voice infused with a blend of curiosity and reverence for cultural diversity. "In today's interconnected world, organizations must navigate a global landscape characterized by diverse cultural norms, values, and practices."

He clicked the remote, and the screen illuminated with the title: **"Cross-cultural Management Philosophies."**

"Our journey continues with the recognition that effective cross-cultural management requires an understanding and appreciation of cultural differences," Michael continued, gesturing towards the screen. "By examining cross-cultural management philosophies, we can develop strategies to harness the power of cultural diversity and foster collaboration across borders."

The screen transitioned to images depicting scenes of cultural exchange, collaboration, and mutual respect in diverse organizational settings. "Our first consideration is the philosophy of **cultural intelligence**. Cultural intelligence emphasizes the ability to understand and adapt to different cultural contexts, communicate effectively across cultural boundaries, and build trust and rapport with individuals from diverse backgrounds."

Michael explained, "By cultivating cultural intelligence, organizations can navigate cultural differences with sensitivity and respect, and leverage cultural diversity as a source of innovation and creativity. Cultural intelligence enables leaders and teams to bridge cultural divides, resolve conflicts, and build meaningful relationships across borders."

The executives nodded in agreement, recognizing the importance of cultural intelligence in today's globalized world.

"Next," Michael said, clicking to the next slide, "let's explore the philosophy of **cultural synergy**. Cultural synergy emphasizes the idea that cultural diversity can be a source of strength and competitive advantage for organizations."

The screen displayed images depicting diverse teams collaborating, brainstorming, and problem-solving together. "Cultural synergy calls for organizations to embrace cultural diversity, foster inclusive work environments, and harness the unique perspectives and talents of individuals from different cultural backgrounds."

Michael continued, "By promoting cultural synergy, organizations can enhance creativity, innovation, and performance, and gain a competitive edge in the global marketplace."

The executives leaned forward, captivated by the idea of cultural synergy as a driver of organizational success in a diverse world.

"Our final consideration," Michael said, "is the philosophy of **cultural relativism**. Cultural relativism emphasizes the importance of respecting cultural differences and recognizing the validity of different cultural norms, values, and practices."

The screen transitioned to visuals depicting cultural relativism in action, with individuals celebrating their cultural heritage and expressing their unique identities. "Cultural relativism challenges us to question our own cultural assumptions and biases, and to approach cross-cultural interactions with humility, curiosity, and empathy."

Michael explained, "By embracing cultural relativism, organizations can foster inclusive workplaces, build trust and collaboration across cultural boundaries, and create environments where individuals feel valued, respected, and empowered to contribute their unique perspectives and talents."

He paused, allowing the significance of cross-cultural management philosophies to resonate with the team. "In conclusion," Michael said, turning off the projector and facing his team, "by examining cross-cultural management philosophies, we can develop strategies to harness the power of cultural diversity and foster collaboration across borders. By cultivating cultural intelligence, promoting cultural synergy, and embracing cultural relativism, we can build organizations that are inclusive, innovative, and successful in a diverse and interconnected world."

With a renewed commitment to understanding and embracing cultural diversity, the executives at Apex Global Consulting prepared to integrate these insights into their management practices, knowing that they held the key to unlocking the full potential of their global workforce and achieving sustainable success in the global marketplace.

Case Studies on Global Ethical Practices

As the executives delved deeper into the intricacies of globalization and management, Michael turned their attention towards real-world examples of global ethical practices. With a sense of anticipation, they prepared to explore case studies that would illuminate the practical applications of ethical principles in a global context.

"Now, let's delve into **case studies on global ethical practices**," Michael declared, his voice carrying a tone of intrigue and anticipation. "These real-world examples will offer valuable insights into how organizations navigate ethical challenges and uphold ethical standards in a globalized world."

He clicked the remote, and the screen illuminated with the title: **"Case Studies on Global Ethical Practices."**

"Our journey continues with a series of case studies that highlight exemplary ethical practices in global business operations," Michael continued, gesturing towards the screen. "By examining these case studies, we can gain valuable lessons and inspiration for our own ethical endeavors in the global marketplace."

The screen transitioned to images depicting scenes of ethical leadership, integrity, and social responsibility in diverse organizational settings. "Our first case study is that of **Patagonia**, a renowned outdoor apparel company known for its commitment to environmental sustainability and social responsibility."

Michael explained, "Patagonia has implemented a range of initiatives to reduce its environmental footprint, including using recycled materials, minimizing waste, and investing in renewable energy. The company also supports environmental activism and advocates for policies to protect the planet."

The executives nodded in admiration, recognizing Patagonia's leadership in ethical business practices.

"Next," Michael said, clicking to the next slide, "let's explore the case of **Unilever**, a multinational consumer goods company that has made sustainability a core part of its business strategy."

The screen displayed images depicting Unilever's efforts to promote sustainable sourcing, reduce greenhouse gas emissions, and improve the livelihoods of smallholder farmers in developing countries. "Unilever's Sustainable Living Plan sets ambitious targets for reducing environmental impact, improving health and well-being, and enhancing livelihoods, demonstrating the company's commitment to creating a more sustainable future."

The executives leaned forward, captivated by Unilever's ambitious sustainability initiatives.

"Our final case study," Michael said, "is that of **TOMS Shoes**, a social enterprise that has revolutionized the concept of corporate social responsibility through its 'One for One' model."

The screen transitioned to visuals depicting TOMS Shoes' mission to provide a pair of shoes to a child in need for every pair purchased, as well as its initiatives to address other social issues such as clean water access and eye care. "TOMS Shoes has demonstrated that it's possible for businesses to be profitable while making a positive social impact, inspiring a new generation of socially conscious consumers and entrepreneurs."

He paused, allowing the significance of these case studies on global ethical practices to resonate with the team. "In conclusion," Michael said, turning off the projector and facing his team, "by examining these case studies, we can gain valuable insights into how organizations navigate ethical challenges and uphold ethical standards in a globalized world. By following the examples set by companies like Patagonia, Unilever, and TOMS Shoes, we can aspire to create positive change in our own organizations and contribute to a more ethical and sustainable future for all."

With a renewed sense of purpose and inspiration, the executives at Apex Global Consulting prepared to draw upon the lessons learned from these case studies to guide their own ethical endeavors in the global marketplace, knowing that they held the key to shaping a future that is not only successful but also ethical, responsible, and socially impactful.

Strategies for Ethical Global Management

As the executives continued their exploration of globalization and management, Michael shifted their focus towards formulating effective strategies for ethical global management. With a sense of urgency, they prepared to devise actionable plans to navigate the complex landscape of global business while upholding ethical standards.

"Now, let's discuss **strategies for ethical global management**," Michael declared, his voice resonating with determination and purpose. "In an interconnected world, organizations must proactively address ethical challenges and ensure that their global operations are conducted with integrity and responsibility."

He clicked the remote, and the screen illuminated with the title: "**Strategies for Ethical Global Management.**"

"Our journey continues with the recognition that ethical global management requires a comprehensive approach that encompasses policies, practices, and culture," Michael continued, gesturing towards the screen. "By implementing these strategies, organizations can foster a culture of ethics and responsibility that guides their actions in every corner of the globe."

The screen transitioned to images depicting scenes of ethical leadership, transparency, and accountability in diverse organizational settings. "Our first strategy is to **embed ethics into the organizational culture**. Ethical values should be integrated into every aspect of the organization, from hiring and training to decision-making and performance evaluation."

Michael explained, "By fostering a culture of ethics, organizations can create an environment where employees feel empowered to speak up about ethical concerns, where ethical behavior is recognized and rewarded, and where leaders lead by example in upholding ethical standards."

The executives nodded in agreement, recognizing the importance of embedding ethics into the fabric of their organization's culture.

"Next," Michael said, clicking to the next slide, "let's explore the strategy of **establishing clear ethical guidelines and policies**. Organizations must develop and communicate clear policies and guidelines that outline expected behavior, ethical standards, and procedures for addressing ethical dilemmas."

The screen displayed images depicting examples of ethical guidelines and policies, including codes of conduct, whistleblowing procedures, and conflict of interest policies. "By establishing clear ethical guidelines and policies, organizations provide employees with the guidance and support they need to make ethical decisions and navigate complex ethical situations."

The executives leaned forward, captivated by the idea of clear ethical guidelines as a roadmap for ethical behavior.

"Our final strategy," Michael said, "is to **promote transparency and accountability**. Organizations must be transparent about their business practices, performance, and impact on society and the environment."

The screen transitioned to visuals depicting examples of transparency and accountability, including sustainability reports, stakeholder engagement initiatives, and mechanisms for receiving feedback and complaints. "By promoting transparency and accountability, organizations build trust and credibility with stakeholders, demonstrate their commitment to ethical behavior, and invite scrutiny and feedback from external parties."

He paused, allowing the significance of these strategies for ethical global management to resonate with the team. "In conclusion," Michael said, turning off the projector and facing his team, "by implementing these strategies for ethical global management, organizations can foster a culture of ethics and responsibility that guides their actions in every corner of the globe. By embedding ethics into the organizational culture, establishing clear ethical guidelines and policies, and promoting transparency and accountability, we can build organizations that are not only successful but also ethical, responsible, and trusted by stakeholders."

With a renewed commitment to ethical global management, the executives at Apex Global Consulting prepared to implement these strategies within their own organization, knowing that they held the key to shaping a future that is not only successful but also ethical, responsible, and sustainable.

Balancing Local and Global Ethics

As the executives delved deeper into the complexities of global management ethics, Michael directed their attention towards the delicate balance between local and global ethical considerations. With a sense of anticipation, they prepared to explore the nuances of navigating ethical dilemmas in diverse cultural contexts.

"Now, let's explore the challenge of **balancing local and global ethics**," Michael declared, his voice tinged with a mixture of contemplation and determination. "In an interconnected world, organizations must navigate the complexities of cultural diversity while upholding universal ethical principles."

He clicked the remote, and the screen illuminated with the title: "**Balancing Local and Global Ethics.**"

"Our journey continues with the recognition that ethical dilemmas often arise when local cultural norms and values conflict with global ethical standards," Michael continued, gesturing towards the screen. "By examining these challenges, we can develop strategies to navigate them with sensitivity, respect, and integrity."

The screen transitioned to images depicting scenes of cultural diversity and ethical dilemmas in global business contexts. "Our first consideration is the importance of **cultural sensitivity**. Organizations must understand and respect the cultural norms, values, and practices of the communities in which they operate."

Michael explained, "By being culturally sensitive, organizations can avoid inadvertently offending or disrespecting local customs and traditions. This requires humility, openness, and a willingness to learn from and collaborate with local stakeholders."

The executives nodded in agreement, recognizing the significance of cultural sensitivity in navigating ethical dilemmas.

"Next," Michael said, clicking to the next slide, "let's explore the concept of **ethical relativism**. Ethical relativism acknowledges that ethical standards may vary across cultures and contexts, and that there is no universal standard of right and wrong."

The screen displayed images depicting examples of ethical relativism in action, including cultural practices and beliefs that may differ from mainstream ethical standards. "While ethical relativism can help organizations understand and respect cultural diversity, it also presents challenges in reconciling conflicting ethical norms and values."

Michael continued, "Organizations must navigate these challenges with care, balancing the need to respect cultural diversity with the imperative to uphold universal ethical principles such as human rights, integrity, and justice."

The executives leaned forward, captivated by the complexities of balancing local and global ethics.

"Our final consideration," Michael said, "is the importance of **ethical leadership**. Leaders must set the tone for ethical behavior and decision-making, both locally and globally."

The screen transitioned to visuals depicting examples of ethical leadership in diverse cultural contexts, including leaders who prioritize integrity, fairness, and transparency in their interactions with employees, customers, and communities. "Ethical leaders foster a culture of ethics and responsibility that guides organizational behavior and decision-making in every corner of the globe."

He paused, allowing the significance of balancing local

and global ethics to resonate with the team. "In conclusion," Michael said, turning off the projector and facing his team, "by balancing local and global ethics, organizations can navigate the complexities of cultural diversity while upholding universal ethical principles. By being culturally sensitive, embracing ethical relativism with caution, and fostering ethical leadership, we can build organizations that are not only successful but also ethical, respectful, and trusted by stakeholders."

With a renewed commitment to navigating ethical dilemmas with sensitivity and integrity, the executives at Apex Global Consulting prepared to integrate these insights into their management practices, knowing that they held the key to shaping a future that is not only successful but also ethical, responsible, and inclusive.

Chapter 15: The Future of Philosophical Management

Emerging Trends in Philosophical Management

As the executives gathered to discuss the future of philosophical management, Michael set the stage for an exploration of emerging trends that would shape the landscape of organizational leadership and ethics. With a sense of anticipation, they prepared to peer into the crystal ball of tomorrow's management practices.

"Welcome, everyone, to our discussion on **the future of philosophical management**," Michael announced, his voice carrying a tone of excitement and curiosity. "As we look ahead, it's important to consider the emerging trends that will influence how organizations approach leadership, ethics, and decision-making."

He clicked the remote, and the screen illuminated with the title: "**Emerging Trends in Philosophical Management.**"

"Our journey into the future begins with a recognition of the dynamic nature of organizational management," Michael continued, gesturing towards the screen. "By examining these emerging trends, we can prepare ourselves to navigate the complexities of tomorrow's business landscape with wisdom and foresight."

The screen transitioned to images depicting scenes of technological innovation, social change, and global interconnectedness. "Our first consideration is the rise of **technological integration**. As advancements in artificial intelligence, automation, and data analytics continue to reshape the way we work, organizations must grapple with ethical questions surrounding privacy, security, and human dignity."

Michael explained, "Philosophical management will play a crucial role in guiding organizations through these technological transformations, ensuring that they harness the power of technology for good while minimizing its negative impacts on society and the environment."

The executives nodded in agreement, recognizing the significance of ethical leadership in the age of rapid technological change.

"Next," Michael said, clicking to the next slide, "let's explore the trend towards **purpose-driven leadership**. In an era characterized by increasing social and environmental challenges, organizations are shifting towards a more purpose-driven approach to leadership, prioritizing values such as sustainability, social responsibility, and human well-being."

The screen displayed images depicting examples of purpose-driven leadership in action, including CEOs who advocate for social justice, environmental stewardship, and economic equality. "By aligning their business strategies with a higher purpose, organizations can inspire their employees, engage their customers, and make a positive impact on society and the planet."

The executives leaned forward, captivated by the potential

of purpose-driven leadership to drive meaningful change.

"Our final consideration," Michael said, "is the growing importance of **global collaboration**. In an increasingly interconnected world, organizations must collaborate across borders and cultures to address complex global challenges such as climate change, poverty, and inequality."

The screen transitioned to visuals depicting examples of global collaboration in action, including partnerships between businesses, governments, and civil society organizations to advance shared goals and address common challenges. "By embracing a philosophy of global collaboration, organizations can leverage the collective wisdom, resources, and expertise of diverse stakeholders to create a more just, sustainable, and prosperous world for all."

He paused, allowing the significance of these emerging trends in philosophical management to resonate with the team. "In conclusion," Michael said, turning off the projector and facing his team, "by embracing these emerging trends in philosophical management, organizations can prepare themselves to navigate the complexities of tomorrow's business landscape with wisdom, foresight, and integrity. By harnessing the power of technology for good, embracing purpose-driven leadership, and fostering global collaboration, we can build organizations that are not only successful but also ethical, responsible, and resilient in the face of change."

With a renewed sense of purpose and vision, the executives at Apex Global Consulting prepared to embrace these emerging trends and lead their organization into a future that is not only successful but also meaningful, sustainable, and socially responsible.

The Role of Technology in Ethical Management

As the executives delved deeper into the future of philosophical management, Michael directed their attention towards the evolving role of technology in shaping ethical management practices. With a sense of urgency, they prepared to explore the intersection of technology and ethics in the organizational landscape of tomorrow.

"Now, let's delve into **the role of technology in ethical management**," Michael declared, his voice tinged with a mixture of contemplation and determination. "In an era of rapid technological advancement, organizations must grapple with the ethical implications of new technologies and harness their potential for good."

He clicked the remote, and the screen illuminated with the title: **"The Role of Technology in Ethical Management."**

"Our journey continues with a recognition of the transformative power of technology," Michael continued, gesturing towards the screen. "By examining the intersection of technology and ethics, we can prepare ourselves to navigate the complexities of tomorrow's digital landscape with wisdom and foresight."

The screen transitioned to images depicting scenes of technological innovation, digital transformation, and ethical decision-making. "Our first consideration is the importance of **ethical design and development**. As organizations embrace new technologies such as artificial intelligence, machine learning, and automation, they must ensure that these technologies are designed and developed with ethical considerations in mind."

Michael explained, "Ethical design and development involves considering the potential impacts of technology on individuals, society, and the environment, and taking proactive steps to mitigate risks and safeguard against unintended consequences."

The executives nodded in agreement, recognizing the significance of ethical design in shaping the future of technology.

"Next," Michael said, clicking to the next slide, "let's explore the concept of **digital ethics**. In an increasingly digital world, organizations must grapple with ethical questions surrounding data privacy, security, and governance."

The screen displayed images depicting examples of digital ethics in action, including organizations that prioritize transparency, accountability, and user consent in their handling of data. "By adopting principles of digital ethics, organizations can build trust with their stakeholders, protect the rights and interests of individuals, and ensure the responsible use of technology."

The executives leaned forward, captivated by the potential of digital ethics to guide responsible technological innovation.

"Our final consideration," Michael said, "is the role of technology in **enhancing ethical decision-making**. As organizations collect and analyze vast amounts of data, they have the opportunity to leverage technology to support ethical decision-making processes."

The screen transitioned to visuals depicting examples of technology-enabled ethical decision-making tools, including algorithms that flag potential ethical risks and assist managers in evaluating the ethical implications of their decisions. "By harnessing the power of technology, organizations can augment human judgment, promote transparency and accountability, and ensure that ethical considerations are integrated into every aspect of decision-making."

He paused, allowing the significance of technology's role in ethical management to resonate with the team. "In conclusion," Michael said, turning off the projector and facing his team, "by embracing technology in ethical management, organizations can leverage the transformative power of technology to advance ethical principles and practices. By prioritizing ethical design and development, adopting principles of digital ethics, and leveraging technology to enhance ethical decision-making, we can build organizations that are not only successful but also ethical, responsible, and trusted by stakeholders."

With a renewed commitment to embracing technology in ethical management, the executives at Apex Global Consulting prepared to integrate these insights into their organizational practices, knowing that they held the key to shaping a future that is not only technologically advanced but also ethical, responsible, and sustainable.

Preparing for Future Ethical Challenges

As the executives continued their discussion on the future of philosophical management, Michael shifted their focus towards preparing for the ethical challenges that lay ahead. With a sense of urgency, they prepared to confront the uncertainties of tomorrow's business landscape with foresight and resilience.

"Now, let's turn our attention to **preparing for future ethical challenges**," Michael declared, his voice carrying a tone of anticipation and determination. "In an ever-evolving world, organizations must anticipate and address emerging ethical dilemmas to navigate the complexities of tomorrow's business environment."

He clicked the remote, and the screen illuminated with the title: **"Preparing for Future Ethical Challenges."**

"Our journey into the future requires us to confront the unknown with courage and conviction," Michael continued, gesturing towards the screen. "By examining potential ethical challenges, we can equip ourselves to respond with wisdom, integrity, and resilience."

The screen transitioned to images depicting scenes of uncertainty, disruption, and ethical dilemmas in diverse organizational settings. "Our first consideration is the need to **anticipate emerging ethical dilemmas**. As technology, globalization, and social change continue to transform the business landscape, new ethical challenges will inevitably arise."

Michael explained, "Organizations must engage in proactive scenario planning and risk assessment to identify potential ethical dilemmas and develop strategies to address them before they escalate into crises."

The executives nodded in agreement, recognizing the importance of foresight in preparing for future ethical challenges.

"Next," Michael said, clicking to the next slide, "let's explore the concept of **building ethical resilience**. In a rapidly changing world, organizations must cultivate the resilience to adapt and respond to ethical challenges with agility and integrity."

The screen displayed images depicting examples of ethical resilience in action, including organizations that prioritize ethical leadership, transparency, and accountability in times of crisis. "By fostering a culture of ethics and responsibility, organizations can build the trust and credibility needed to weather storms and emerge stronger on the other side."

The executives leaned forward, captivated by the idea of ethical resilience as a cornerstone of organizational success.

"Our final consideration," Michael said, "is the importance of **continuous learning and adaptation**. In a world of constant change, organizations must embrace a philosophy of lifelong learning and adaptation to stay ahead of the curve."

The screen transitioned to visuals depicting examples of organizations that invest in employee training, leadership development, and knowledge sharing to foster a culture of learning and innovation. "By empowering employees to continuously learn, grow, and adapt, organizations can cultivate the agility and creativity needed to navigate ethical challenges and seize new opportunities."

He paused, allowing the significance of preparing for future ethical challenges to resonate with the team. "In conclusion," Michael said, turning off the projector and facing his team, "by preparing for future ethical challenges, organizations can equip themselves to navigate the complexities of tomorrow's business environment with wisdom, integrity, and resilience. By anticipating emerging ethical dilemmas, building ethical resilience, and embracing continuous learning and adaptation, we can build organizations that are not only successful but also ethical, responsible, and prepared to thrive in an uncertain future."

With a renewed commitment to preparing for future ethical challenges, the executives at Apex Global Consulting prepared to integrate these insights into their organizational practices, knowing that they held the key to shaping a future that is not only successful but also ethical, responsible, and resilient.

CHAPTER 15: THE FUTURE OF PHILOSOPHICAL MANAGEMENT

Philosophical Education for Future Leaders

As the executives delved further into the future of philosophical management, Michael redirected their attention towards the importance of philosophical education for shaping the leaders of tomorrow. With a sense of urgency, they prepared to explore how cultivating philosophical insight could equip future leaders with the wisdom and integrity needed to navigate the complexities of tomorrow's business landscape.

"Now, let's consider the role of **philosophical education for future leaders**," Michael announced, his voice resonating with a tone of conviction and purpose. "In an ever-changing world, organizations must invest in developing leaders who possess not only technical expertise but also philosophical insight."

He clicked the remote, and the screen illuminated with the title: **"Philosophical Education for Future Leaders."**

"Our journey into the future requires us to cultivate leaders who are not only competent but also ethical, empathetic, and visionary," Michael continued, gesturing towards the screen. "By investing in philosophical education, we can nurture the next generation of leaders who possess the wisdom and integrity needed to navigate the complexities of tomorrow's business environment."

The screen transitioned to images depicting scenes of leadership development, philosophical inquiry, and ethical reflection. "Our first consideration is the importance of **integrating philosophy into leadership education**. Aspiring leaders must be exposed to philosophical concepts and principles that can help them develop a deeper understanding of ethics, values, and human nature."

Michael explained, "Philosophical education provides future leaders with the critical thinking skills, moral reasoning abilities, and ethical insights needed to make principled decisions and lead with integrity."

The executives nodded in agreement, recognizing the transformative potential of philosophical education for shaping the leaders of tomorrow.

"Next," Michael said, clicking to the next slide, "let's explore the concept of **ethics training and moral development**. In addition to academic education, future leaders must engage in practical training and moral development activities that cultivate ethical awareness, empathy, and compassion."

The screen displayed images depicting examples of ethics training programs, leadership workshops, and experiential learning opportunities designed to foster ethical leadership skills. "By providing opportunities for reflection, dialogue, and ethical decision-making, organizations can empower future leaders to lead with authenticity, empathy, and moral courage."

The executives leaned forward, captivated by the idea of ethics training as a cornerstone of leadership development.

"Our final consideration," Michael said, "is the importance of **mentoring and role modeling**. In addition to formal education and training, future leaders must have access to mentors and role models who embody the values and principles of ethical leadership."

The screen transitioned to visuals depicting examples of mentorship programs, leadership coaching sessions, and peer support networks designed to provide guidance, support, and inspiration to emerging leaders. "By fostering a culture of mentorship and role modeling, organizations can create a supportive environment where future leaders can learn from the wisdom and experience of others."

He paused, allowing the significance of philosophical education for future leaders to resonate with the team. "In conclusion," Michael said, turning off the projector and facing his team, "by investing in philosophical education for future leaders, organizations can nurture a new generation of leaders who possess the wisdom, integrity, and vision needed to navigate the complexities of tomorrow's business environment. By integrating philosophy into leadership education, providing ethics training and moral development opportunities, and fostering mentoring and role modeling, we can build organizations that are not only successful but also ethical, responsible, and inspiring to others."

With a renewed commitment to investing in philosophical education for future leaders, the executives at Apex Global Consulting prepared to integrate these insights into their leadership development programs, knowing that they held the key to shaping a future that is not only successful but also ethical, responsible, and transformative.

Case Studies on Forward-Thinking Organizations

As the executives delved deeper into the future of philosophical management, Michael directed their attention towards case studies of forward-thinking organizations that exemplified the principles of ethical leadership, innovation, and sustainability. With a sense of anticipation, they prepared to explore real-world examples of organizations that were leading the way towards a more ethical and responsible future.

"Now, let's examine **case studies on forward-thinking**

organizations," Michael declared, his voice resonating with a tone of excitement and curiosity. "In our exploration of the future of philosophical management, it's important to learn from the successes and challenges of organizations that are pioneering new approaches to leadership, ethics, and sustainability."

He clicked the remote, and the screen illuminated with the title: "**Case Studies on Forward-Thinking Organizations.**"

"Our journey into the future continues with a closer look at organizations that are leading by example," Michael continued, gesturing towards the screen. "By examining their strategies, practices, and outcomes, we can gain valuable insights into how to navigate the complexities of tomorrow's business environment with wisdom, integrity, and innovation."

The screen transitioned to images depicting scenes of diverse organizations, ranging from startups to multinational corporations, that were making a positive impact on society and the environment. "Our first case study is **GreenTech Innovations**, a startup that is revolutionizing the renewable energy industry with its innovative solar panel technology."

Michael explained, "By harnessing the power of solar energy to provide clean, affordable electricity to communities around the world, GreenTech Innovations is not only driving environmental sustainability but also promoting economic development and social equity."

The executives nodded in agreement, recognizing the importance of innovation in addressing global challenges.

"Next," Michael said, clicking to the next slide, "let's explore the case of **FairTrade Enterprises**, a global network of businesses that are committed to promoting fair wages, safe working conditions, and environmental sustainability in their

CHAPTER 15: THE FUTURE OF PHILOSOPHICAL MANAGEMENT

supply chains."

The screen displayed images depicting examples of FairTrade Enterprises in action, including coffee cooperatives, textile factories, and agricultural producers that were empowering farmers and workers to build better lives for themselves and their families. "By prioritizing social responsibility and ethical business practices, FairTrade Enterprises is proving that profitability and purpose can go hand in hand."

The executives leaned forward, captivated by the impact of FairTrade Enterprises on global supply chains.

"Our final case study," Michael said, "is **InnovateCorp**, a multinational corporation that is leveraging technology and innovation to address pressing social and environmental challenges."

The screen transitioned to visuals depicting examples of InnovateCorp's initiatives, including projects to reduce carbon emissions, promote diversity and inclusion, and support community development. "By embedding sustainability into its business model and operations, InnovateCorp is demonstrating that large corporations have a responsibility to use their resources and influence for the greater good."

He paused, allowing the significance of case studies on forward-thinking organizations to resonate with the team. "In conclusion," Michael said, turning off the projector and facing his team, "by studying these forward-thinking organizations, we can gain valuable insights into how to navigate the complexities of tomorrow's business environment with wisdom, integrity, and innovation. By learning from their successes and challenges, we can build organizations that are not only successful but also ethical, responsible, and inspiring to others."

With a renewed commitment to learning from the experiences of forward-thinking organizations, the executives at Apex Global Consulting prepared to integrate these insights into their own organizational practices, knowing that they held the key to shaping a future that is not only successful but also ethical, responsible, and sustainable.

Concluding Thoughts and Future Directions

As the executives neared the conclusion of their exploration into the future of philosophical management, Michael guided their focus towards reflecting on the insights gained and charting a course for future directions. With a sense of reflection and anticipation, they prepared to distill their learnings into actionable steps that would shape the trajectory of their organization in the years to come.

"Now, as we approach the end of our journey, let's take a moment to reflect on **concluding thoughts and future directions**," Michael announced, his voice imbued with a blend of introspection and optimism. "In our exploration of the future of philosophical management, we have uncovered valuable insights and lessons that will guide us as we navigate the complexities of tomorrow's business environment."

He clicked the remote, and the screen illuminated with the title: **"Concluding Thoughts and Future Directions."**

"Our journey into the future has been marked by discovery, dialogue, and growth," Michael continued, gesturing towards the screen. "As we conclude our exploration, it's important to distill our learnings into actionable steps that will propel us forward on our quest to build organizations that are not only successful but also ethical, responsible, and sustainable."

CHAPTER 15: THE FUTURE OF PHILOSOPHICAL MANAGEMENT

The screen transitioned to images depicting scenes of collaboration, innovation, and purpose-driven leadership. "Our first consideration is the importance of **integrating ethics into every aspect of our organization**. From leadership development to decision-making processes, from supply chain management to customer relations, ethics must be at the forefront of everything we do."

Michael explained, "By fostering a culture of ethics and responsibility, we can create an organizational environment where integrity, honesty, and accountability are valued and upheld."

The executives nodded in agreement, recognizing the significance of embedding ethics into the DNA of their organization.

"Next," Michael said, clicking to the next slide, "let's explore the concept of **embracing innovation and change**. In a rapidly evolving world, organizations must be agile, adaptable, and open to new ideas and perspectives."

The screen displayed images depicting examples of organizations that embraced innovation and change, including startups that disrupted traditional industries, established companies that reinvented themselves for the digital age, and social enterprises that pioneered new approaches to solving complex problems. "By embracing innovation and change, we can stay ahead of the curve and seize new opportunities for growth and impact."

The executives leaned forward, captivated by the potential of innovation to drive organizational success.

"Our final consideration," Michael said, "is the importance of **continuing our journey of learning and growth**. In a world of constant change, learning is not a destination but a lifelong journey."

The screen transitioned to visuals depicting examples of learning initiatives, knowledge-sharing platforms, and professional development opportunities designed to foster a culture of continuous learning and growth. "By investing in our people, fostering collaboration and creativity, and embracing new ideas and perspectives, we can build an organization that is not only successful but also resilient, adaptive, and future-ready."

He paused, allowing the significance of concluding thoughts and future directions to resonate with the team. "In conclusion," Michael said, turning off the projector and facing his team, "as we embark on the next phase of our journey, let us carry forward the insights and lessons we have gained, and let us continue to strive towards building organizations that are not only successful but also ethical, responsible, and sustainable. By integrating ethics into every aspect of our organization, embracing innovation and change, and fostering a culture of learning and growth, we can chart a course for a future that is not only bright but also full of promise and possibility."

With a renewed sense of purpose and direction, the executives at Apex Global Consulting prepared to embark on the next phase of their journey, knowing that they held the key to shaping a future that is not only successful but also ethical, responsible, and transformative.

About the Author

Goodson Mumba is a multifaceted individual known for his diverse expertise and prolific contributions across various fields. As an infopreneur, thought leader, and spiritual leader, he has inspired countless individuals through his insightful teachings and impactful writings. Mumba is also an accomplished author, with several notable works to his name, including "Understanding Corporate Worship," "The Years I Spent in a Week," "Management By Harmony," "The CEO's Diary," "Change to Change" and "Creative Thinking for results" His literary works span topics ranging from business management to personal development and spirituality, reflecting his broad range of interests and insights.

With a Master of Business Leadership (MBL) and a Bachelor of Arts in Theology (BTh), Mumba brings a unique blend of business acumen and spiritual wisdom to his work. His educational background is further enriched by a Group Diploma in Management Studies, providing him with a solid foundation in organizational dynamics and leadership principles. Additionally, Mumba holds diplomas in Education

Psychology, Leadership and Management Styles, Organizational Behaviour, Financial Accounting, Economic Growth and Development, and Project Management, showcasing his commitment to continuous learning and professional development.

Mumba's expertise extends beyond traditional academic disciplines, encompassing areas such as Neuro-Linguistic Programming (NLP) and Positive Psychology. His diverse skill set is complemented by a range of certifications, including Creative Problem Solving and Decision Making, Life Coaching Fundamentals and Techniques, Professional Life Coaching, and Performance Management System Design. These certifications reflect Mumba's dedication to equipping himself with the tools and knowledge necessary to empower others and drive positive change.

As an author, Mumba's writings reflect his deep understanding of human nature, organizational dynamics, and spiritual principles. His works offer practical insights, actionable strategies, and inspirational guidance for individuals seeking personal growth, professional success, and spiritual fulfillment. Mumba's holistic approach to life and leadership resonates with readers worldwide, making him a respected figure in both the business and spiritual communities.

Overall, Goodson Mumba's diverse background, extensive knowledge, and profound insights make him a sought-after speaker, mentor, and author. His commitment to excellence, lifelong learning, and service to others continues to inspire individuals to unlock their full potential and lead lives of purpose and significance.

Goodson Mumba is renowned for initiating the concept of Management by Harmony, revolutionizing traditional management practices with a focus on balanced and holistic approaches. He has authored two influential books on this subject: "Introduction to Management by Harmony" and its sequel, "Management by Harmony."

Mumba's work has significantly impacted the field, offering innovative strategies for fostering organizational harmony and efficiency. His contributions continue to shape contemporary management theories and practices.

www.ingramcontent.com/pod-product-compliance
Lightning Source LLC
Chambersburg PA
CBHW071826210526
45479CB00001B/12